20 Flamenco Guitar Etudes

Yago Santos

To access the online audio recording go to:
WWW.MELBAY.COM/30997MEB

WWW.MELBAY.COM

Preface

These days, I've noticed that most guitar studies are designed to be more mechanical than melodic, compelling the student to focus on refining a particular left or right-hand pattern.

Practicing this type of study is perhaps the most effective and efficient way of getting into the instrument; as more knowledge is gained, however, it becomes necessary to incorporate a new and more varied daily practice routine in order to achieve a balance between mechanical and interpretive study. To achieve a high level of proficiency, it is vital to invest many hours of study. To do this, we must avoid the monotony of always repeating the same exercises; this is particularly the case when it comes to non-melodic studies. In an effort to sharpen the senses and broaden our musical vocabulary, it is of special interest to introduce unique harmonic progressions (for example by modulating sections) that serve as compositional ideas that ultimately link our study and performance practice.

Once I had come up with these concepts, I got the idea of composing a book of 20 studies that precisely alternate functionality and interpretation for both amateur and professional guitarists. I hope you enjoy and benefit from playing these pieces.

Yago Santos

Contents

Prologue

It is an honor for me to write a few lines as a prologue for this book by Yago Santos.

I met a young piano trained musician in 2009, during one of the lessons I was teaching at the Amor de Dios Flamenco studio in Madrid. There, he appeared with his guitar and I asked him to play something for me. I was immediately captivated by his way of interpreting as well as his personality. Since then, we have consolidated an intense professional as well as personal relationship.

I remember with special affection the presentation concert of my album *Parque de Maria Luisa*, which we performed at the Lope de Vega theater in Seville. During those years Yago had grown a lot, with successful concerts and recitals all over the world to prove it. This musical and personal growth is reflected in this book, which opens new paths for flamenco music through twenty studies of his own authorship. With them, the performer will work tonal and modal harmonies in different keys, as well as practicing different arpeggio systems or techniques such as tremolo, ligado and picado.

Being a musician today engenders something more than charisma; hours of study and rigorous work are essential in the formation of the artist's personality. That is why I recommend this book both to classical and flamenco guitarists.

I hope you enjoy this book as much as I do.

Rafael Riqueni

About the Audio Recording

The 20 studies of the book have been recorded by the author and are available online. The url to access the audio recording is found on the title page of this book. Each of the studies is accompanied by an icon, which indicates its corresponding track number.

PRELIMINARY CONCEPTS

PARTS OF THE GUITAR

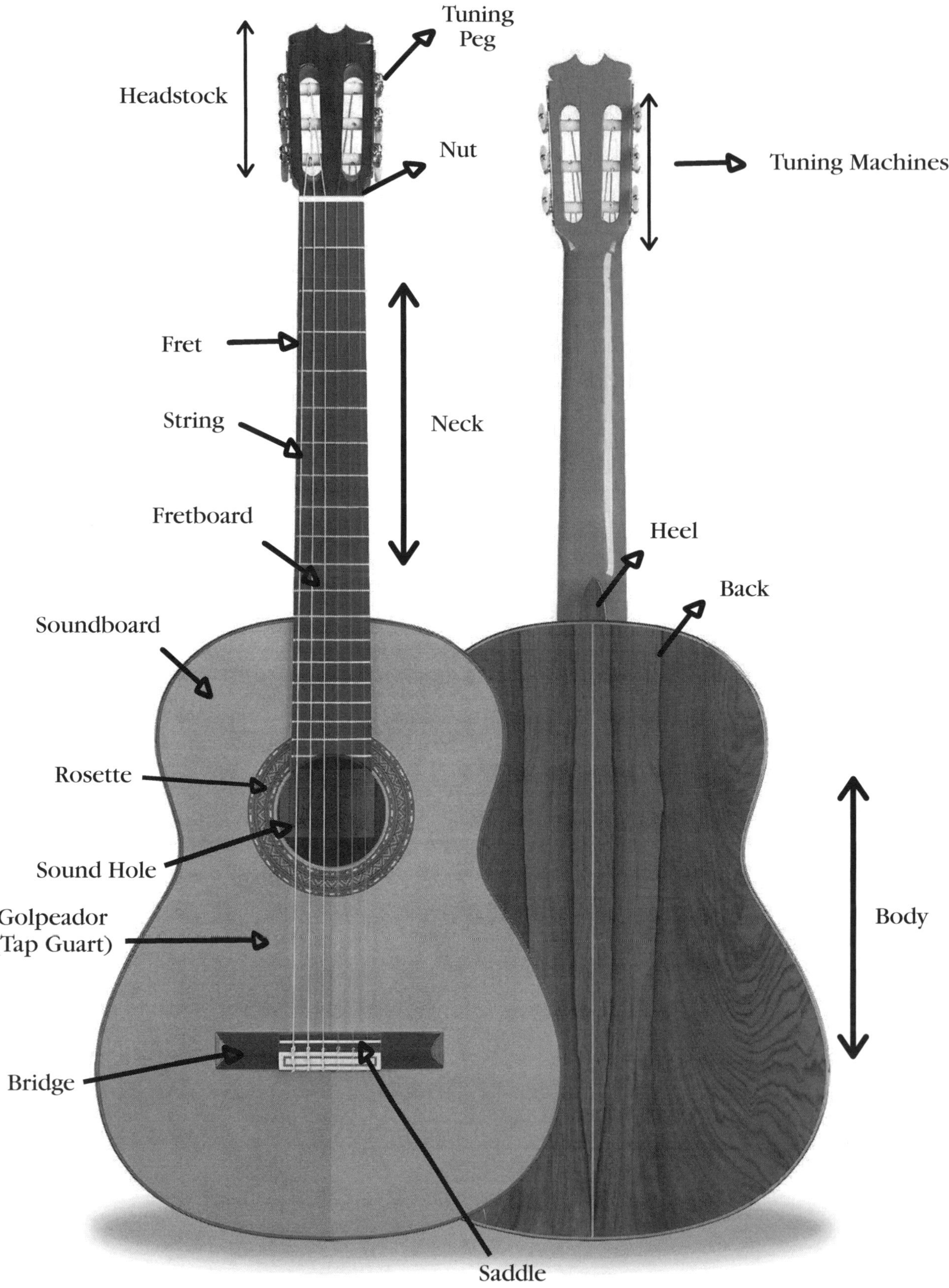

In this fine rosewood guitar, the *golpeador* (tap guard) is not visible, as in most high-end flamenco guitars.

POSTURE AND PERFORMANCE

Traditionally, flamenco guitarists held the guitar by placing it on top of their right leg, supporting it in their left hand, and with both feet on the ground. This position reduces the mobility of the left hand, which is already busy holding the guitar. However, this was not a problem for early flamenco players, who used to play chords and scales only in the first position of the guitar.

Modern flamenco players tend to cross their legs and rest the guitar on the upper part of the right leg, in order to enhance agility and capability in the left hand. Holding the guitar on the right leg frees the left hand; this way, it can move along the fretboard and reach all positions.

The shoulders must be totally relaxed. The right elbow should be placed on top of the guitar so that the right hand can move freely and naturally.

The flamenco guitar is played by placing the right hand between the sound hole and bridge of the guitar, in order to produce a brighter sound. Position your right hand so that the knuckle line is almost parallel to the strings, with the thumb outside the fingers. The hand should be as relaxed as possible. Don't try to force it in any way. Rest your thumb on the sixth string with your fingers perpendicular to the strings. Although it may vary slightly according to the technique being used, your right hand should assume this fixed but relaxed position whenever you are about to play. This will save you a lot of time and effort when executing different guitar techniques.

The left hand should also remain relaxed. Keep the fingertips perpendicular to the fretboard, close to the frets. The thumb and hand remain straight, with a little space between the palm of the hand and the neck of the guitar. The thumb of the left hand should always be centered behind the neck. This helps keep the hand straight and provides greater range of motion to the fingers. It is crucial to develop strength, speed and precision in each of the four fingers of the left hand, for effective use in quick placement and lifting. Keep your right-hand knuckles parallel to the strings of the guitar, allowing the fingers to drop at a right angle to the strings rather than directly across them.

INTERVALS

While it takes a minimum of 3 simultaneous or arpeggiated notes to form a chord, 2 notes played together or sequentially form an interval.* Intervals are named by quality and number, i.e., Major 2nd (M2).

Classification of Intervals

Major and Perfect	Augmented	Minor and Diminished
M2 Major 2nd	♯2 Augmented 2nd (+2)	♭2 flat 2 minor 2nd (m2)
* M9 Major 9th	♯9 Augmented 9th (+9)	♭9 flat 9 minor 9th (m9)
M3 Major 3rd	—	♭3 flat 3 minor 3rd (m3)
* M10 Major 10th	—	♭10 minor 10th (m10)
P4 Perfect 4th	♯4 Augmented 4th Sharp 4 (+4)	—
* P11 Perfect 11th	♯11 Augmented 11th (+11)	—
P5 Perfect 5th	♯5 Augmented 5th Sharp 5 (+5)	♭5 flat 5 or diminished 5th (d5)
M6 Major 6th	—	♭6 flat 6th minor 6th (m6)
* M13 Major 13th	—	♭13 flat 13 minor 13 (m13)
Δ Maj7 Major 7th M7	—	m7 minor 7th

* Compound intervals larger than an octave are named like their counterparts within one octave.

* Intervals can be perfect, major, minor, diminished, or augmented in quality. Unisons, fourths, fifths, and octaves are said to be *perfect* intervals. Major and perfect intervals raised a half step are said to be *augmented*. A major interval lowered a half step becomes minor. Minor and perfect intervals lowered a half step are said to be *diminished*. Intervals may also be doubly augmented or doubly diminished, as in the fully-diminished 7th chord.

CHORD SYMBOLS

Chord symbols are universally expressed by assigning an A-G letter name to the traditional solfage syllables used in sight singing:

Do	Re	Mi	Fa	Sol	La	Si/Ti	Do
C	D	E	F	G	A	B	C

Note that all of these symbols and common chord symbols and formulas are based on the tonic note C.

Chords	Symbols	Member Notes
Major	C	1–3–5
Augmented	C+ Caug	1–3–♯5
Minor	C- Cm Cmin	1–♭3–5
Diminished	C° Cdim	1–♭3–♭5
Major 7th	Cmaj7 CM7 CΔ	1–3–5–Maj7
Half-Diminished 7th	Cm7(♭5) C-7(♭5) Cø7	1–♭3–♭5–♭7
Fully-Diminished 7th	C°7 Cdim7	1–♭3–♭5–♭♭7
Add9	Cadd9	1–3–5–9
Suspended 2nd	Csus2	1–2–5
Suspended 4th	Csus4	1–4–5

The symbols of chords that coincide with the melody are placed above the staff.

THE GUITAR IN SHEET MUSIC

Guitar notation is written one octave higher than it actually sounds, as can be seen in following example:

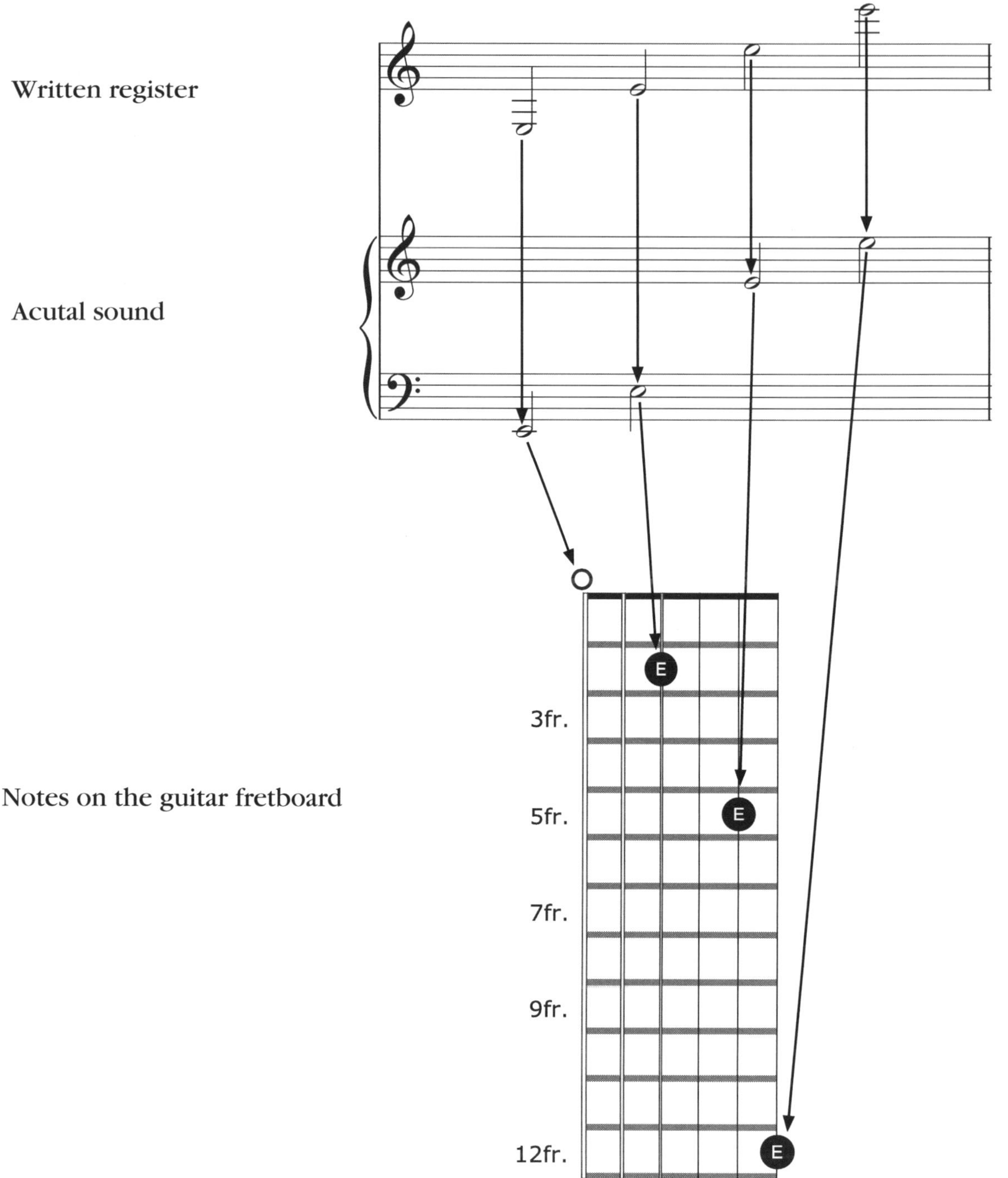

STRATEGIES AND PRACTICE TIPS

Left-Hand Technique

Left-hand technique includes the study of scales, invervals, arpeggios and mechanical exercises.

Right-Hand Technique

Right-hand technique includes arpeggios, picado, pulgar, pulgar-indice (*pi*), trémolo, alzapúa, horquilla, golpe, and rasgueado techniques.

Speed and Precision

The secret to gaining speed and precision is to study slowly and diligently.

Sound

Technique study must be at the service of quality sound, which is at the center of our identity as musical artists.

Expressiveness and Dynamics

Every note is important and has meaning, so play each note expressively.

Improvisation

Improvise over new chord progressions daily.

Accompaniment

Study harmonic and melodic accompaniment.

Harmony

Knowledge of harmony will help you understand what you are playing.

Rhythm

Rhythm is everything.

Composition

The creation and search for our own signature sound and sense of interpretation must be our ultimate goal.

Use a metronome.

The metronome should become your best friend; it will improve your rhythm and correct your tempo inaccruacies.

Be consistent.

Practice the guitar every day; it is better to study 15 minutes a day that an hour a week in one session.

Motivate yourself.

Stay encouraged and motivated every day you pick up the guitar. Establish daily challenges and goals with the guitar that will help you improve.

Studying doesn't have to be boring.

Studying is not boring; it can be fun, depending on how you think about it.

Be creative.

Diversify your study time and be creative; take care that your study should not be something repetitive.

Set clear goals.

Results on the guitar are obtained in the medium and long term, so be patient.

Record your practice every day.

Use a computer, digital or tape recorder to record yourself at the end of each practice session. The next day, before you begin practicing, listen to the previous days recording; that way, you will be aware of your progress and the areas that need improvement.

Examine how you play.

Study as if you are on stage, not mechanically, but rather as you intend to perform before an audience.

Create your own study routine.

Each individual is different and has their own work ethic and sense of musical taste. Adapt the following practice schedule to your own needs.

DAILY CALENDAR AND STUDY ROUTINE

An efficient and well-organized practice routine is one of the best ways to continue improving with the guitar. Due to the lack of free time, establishing an organized practice routine will help you grow as a guitarist.

Setting short and long-term goals for your playing and learning how to break them down will really help you stay on the right track with your playing.

Below is a one-hour daily practice routine including previously mentioned elements. The idea is to take advantage of those 60 minutes in the subjects that you like the most and those that help you get out of your comfort zone. It is very important to dedicate part of your study time to those areas in whick you fell less fluent, as well as to repertoire review.

	MONDAY	TUESDAY	WEDNESDAY	THURSDAY	FRIDAY	SATURDAY
10 MINUTES	Warm-Up	Warm-Up	Warm-Up	Warm-Up	Warm-Up	Warm-Up
20 MINUTES	Technique + Repertoire	Technique + Repertoire	Technique + Repertoire	Technique + Repertoire	Technique + Repertoire	Technique + Repertoire
20 MINUTES	Ear Training	Rhythm Study	Harmony	Comping	Harmony	Rhythm Study
10 MINUTES	Comping	Sightreading	Improvisation	Sightreading	Improvisation	Comping

Sunday will be our day of rest, so choose your favorite subjects from the previous days.

Twenty studies covering the basic guitar techniques are featured in this book.

If you want to learn flamenco pieces, I recommend my books *Alma de Niño Songbook 1* and *Alma de Niño Songbook 2* where you will find transcription of the 15 pieces of my first solo album, *Alma de Niño*.

" The packaging can be important; the content must be." Paco de Lucía

ETUDE I

Warm-Up Study

In this study, the left hand performs extensions while playing variations of the chromatic scale. The same patterns are played on all six strings using *imim* alternation throughout, but it could also be played *mama*, *iaia*, or *imam* if you're feeling adventurous.

"Forget about any other lesson. You have to be able to mark time with your foot or you will not have any control over what you are doing."

Al di Meola

Etude I

Music and transcription by
YAGO SANTOS

Presto ♩=148

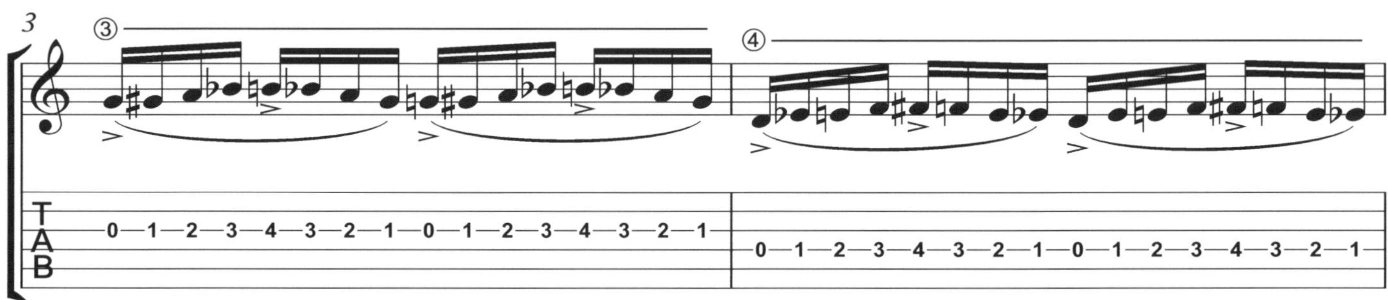

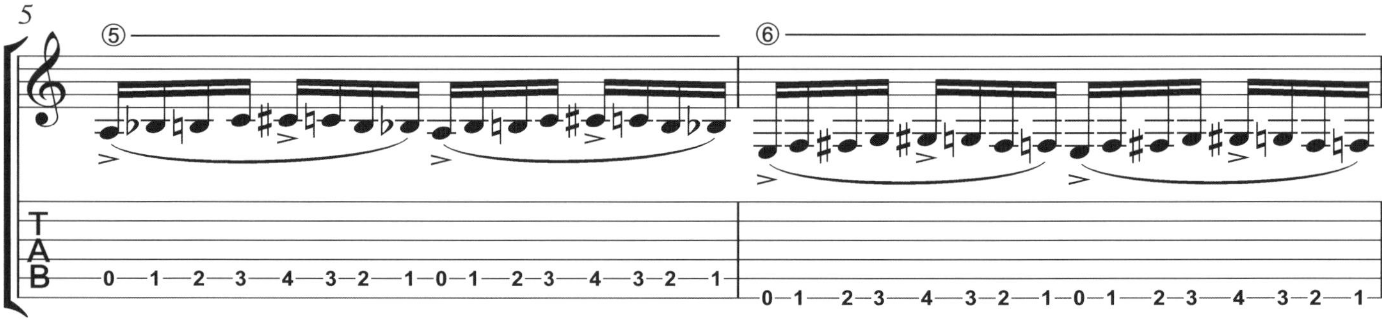

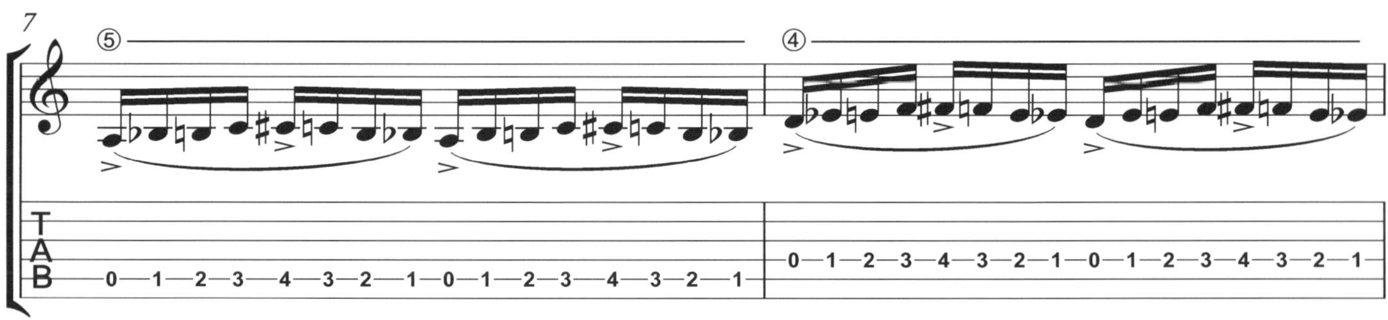

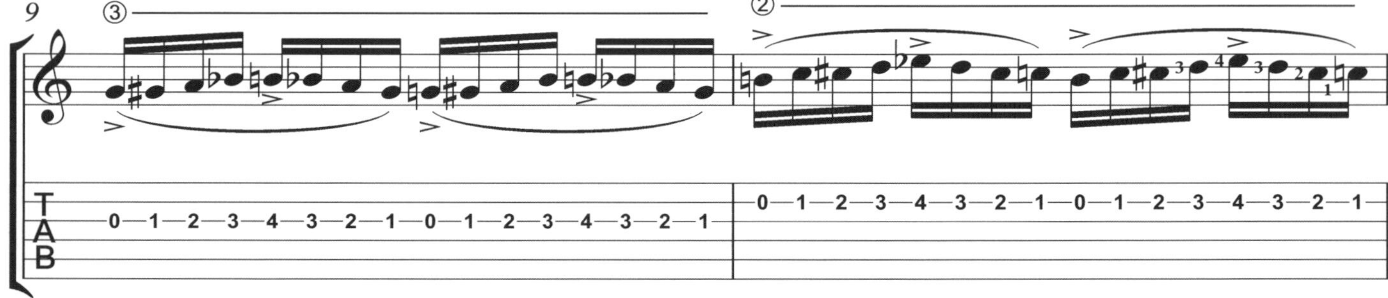

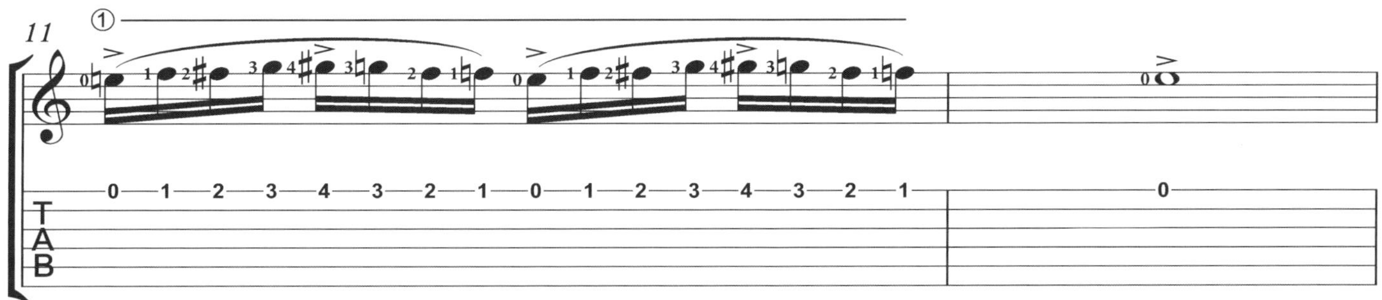

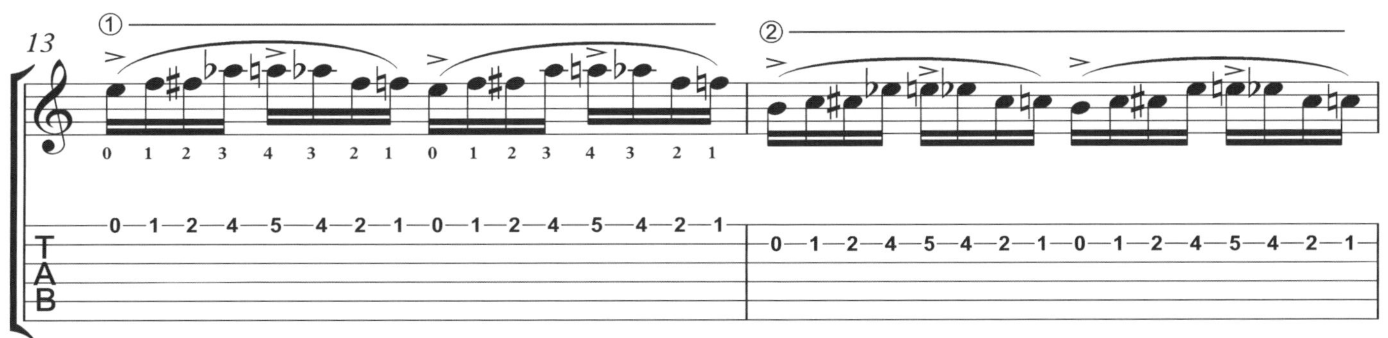

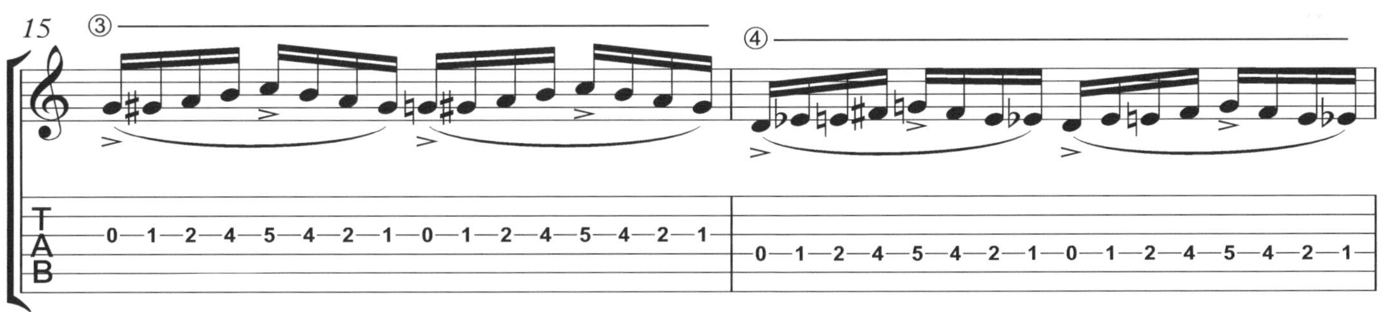

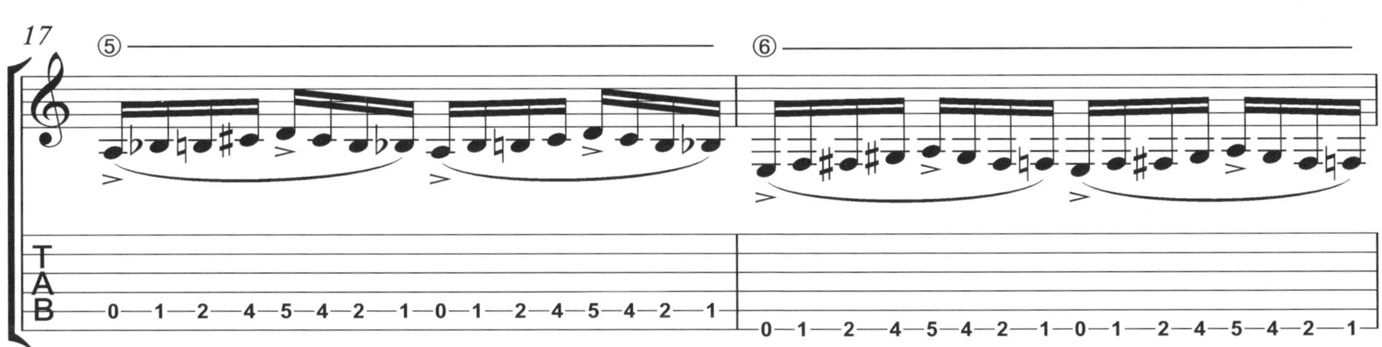

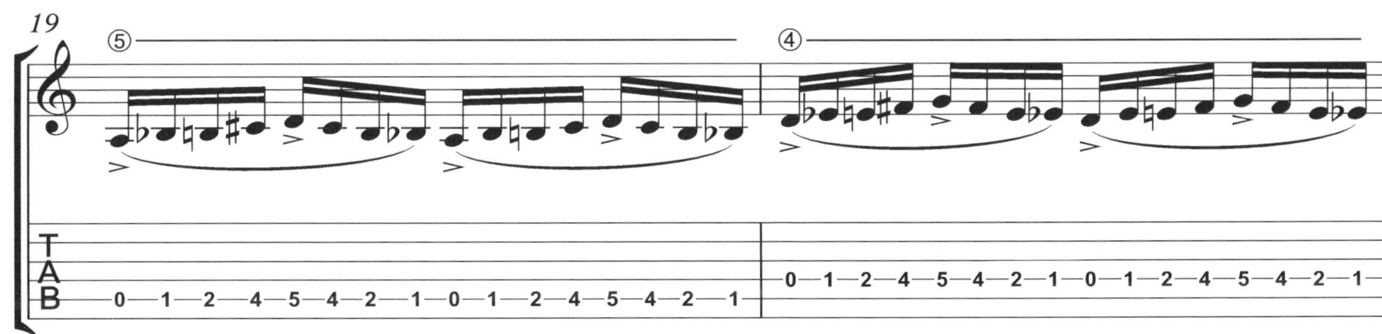

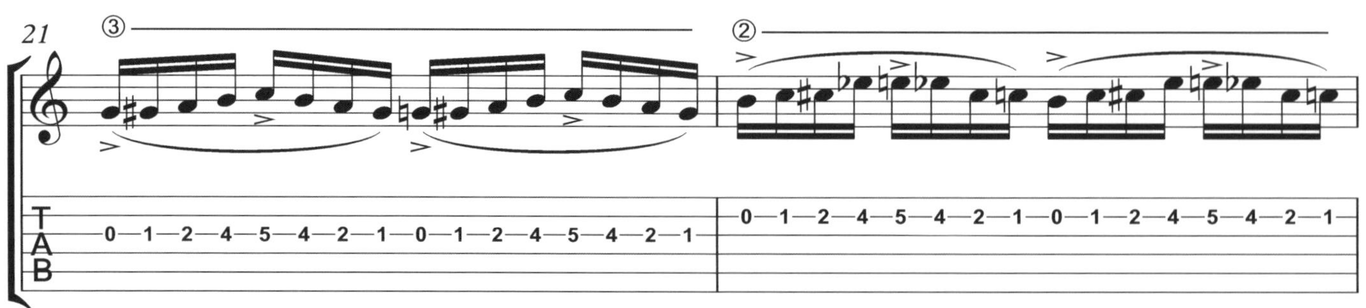
21
③
②
T
A
B
0—1—2—4—5—4—2—1—0—1—2—4—5—4—2—1
0—1—2—4—5—4—2—1—0—1—2—4—5—4—2—1

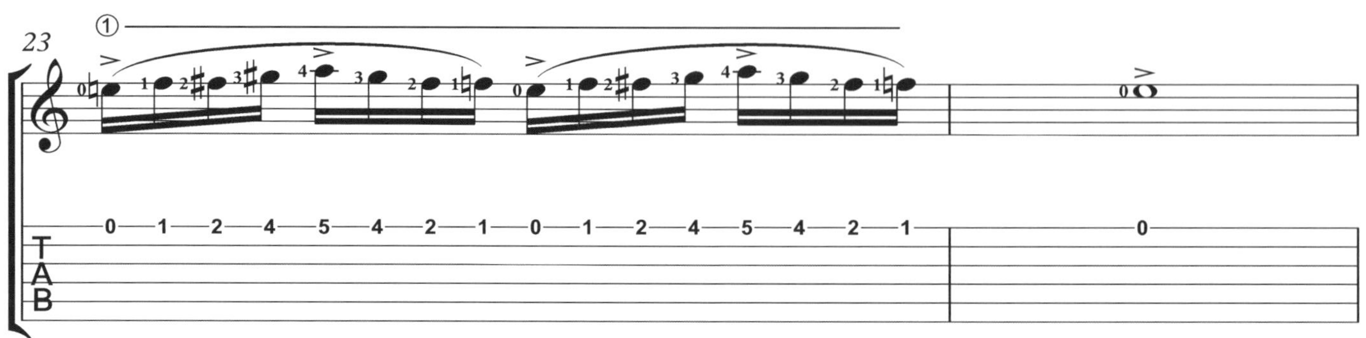
23
①
T
A
B
0—1—2—4—5—4—2—1—0—1—2—4—5—4—2—1
0

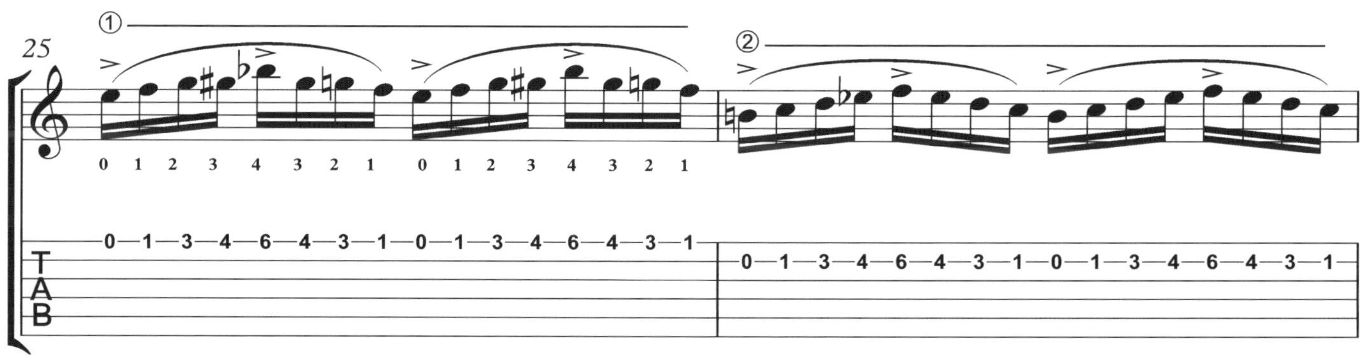
25
①
②
0 1 2 3 4 3 2 1 0 1 2 3 4 3 2 1
T
A
B
0—1—3—4—6—4—3—1—0—1—3—4—6—4—3—1
0—1—3—4—6—4—3—1—0—1—3—4—6—4—3—1

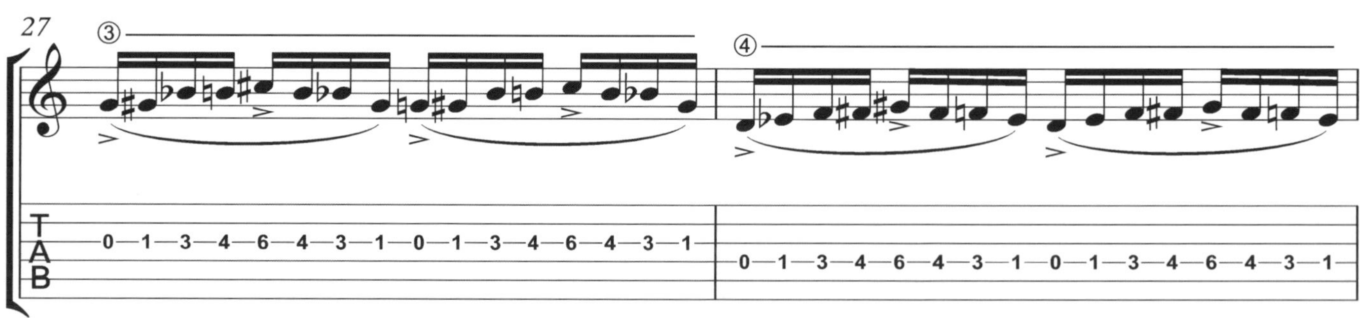
27
③
④
T
A
B
0—1—3—4—6—4—3—1—0—1—3—4—6—4—3—1
0—1—3—4—6—4—3—1—0—1—3—4—6—4—3—1

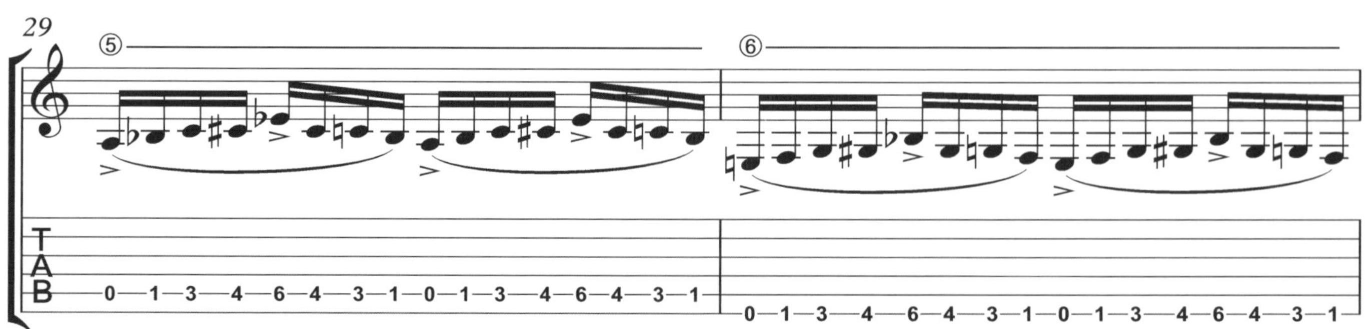
29
⑤
⑥
T
A
B
0—1—3—4—6—4—3—1—0—1—3—4—6—4—3—1
0—1—3—4—6—4—3—1—0—1—3—4—6—4—3—1

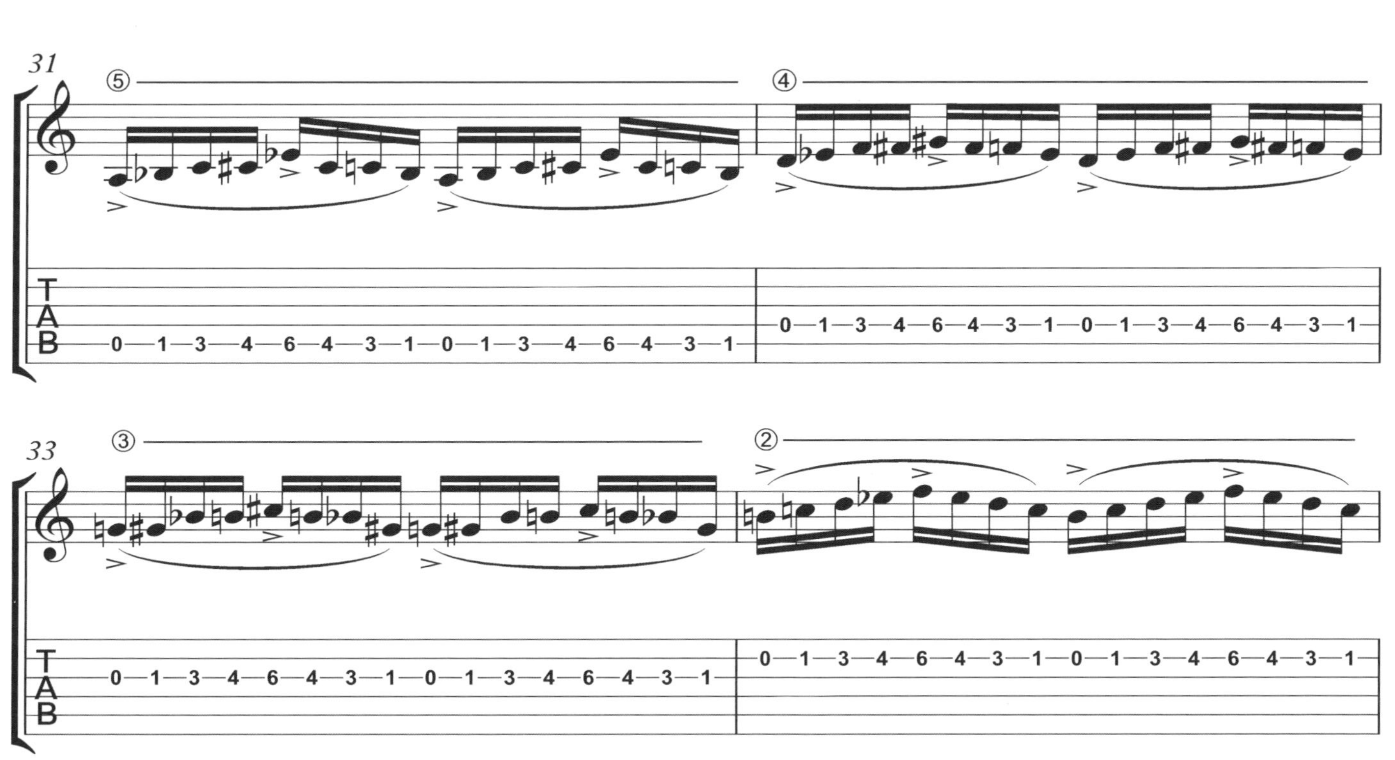
31
TAB
33
TAB

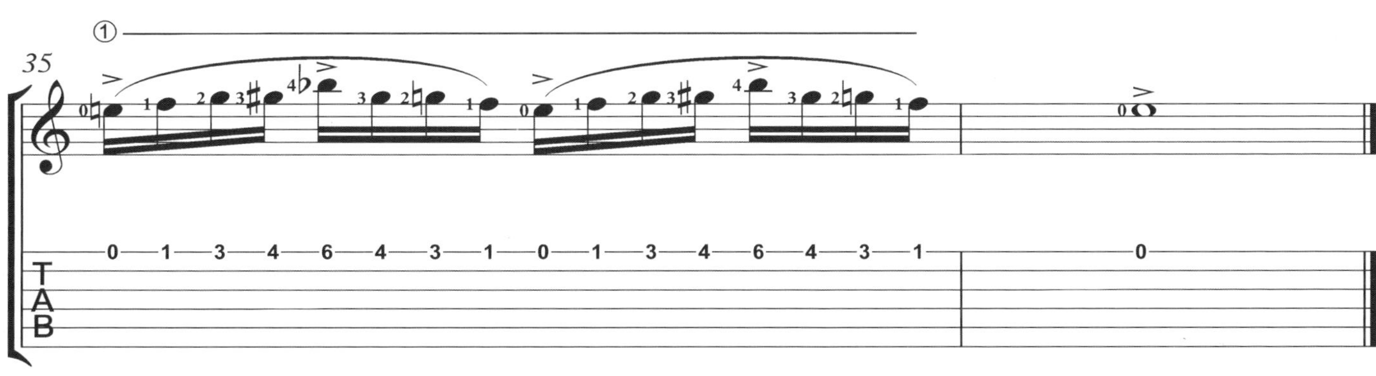
35
TAB

ETUDE II

Interval Study

You will practice thirds and fourths, both natural and repetitive.
This will help you improve your phrasing and gain agility with your left hand.

"One day you pick up the guitar and you feel like a great teacher, and the next day you feel like a fool. It is because we are different every day, but the guitar is always the same ... wonderful."

Tommy Emmanuel

2

Etude II

Tempo ♩=120

Music and transcription by
YAGO SANTOS

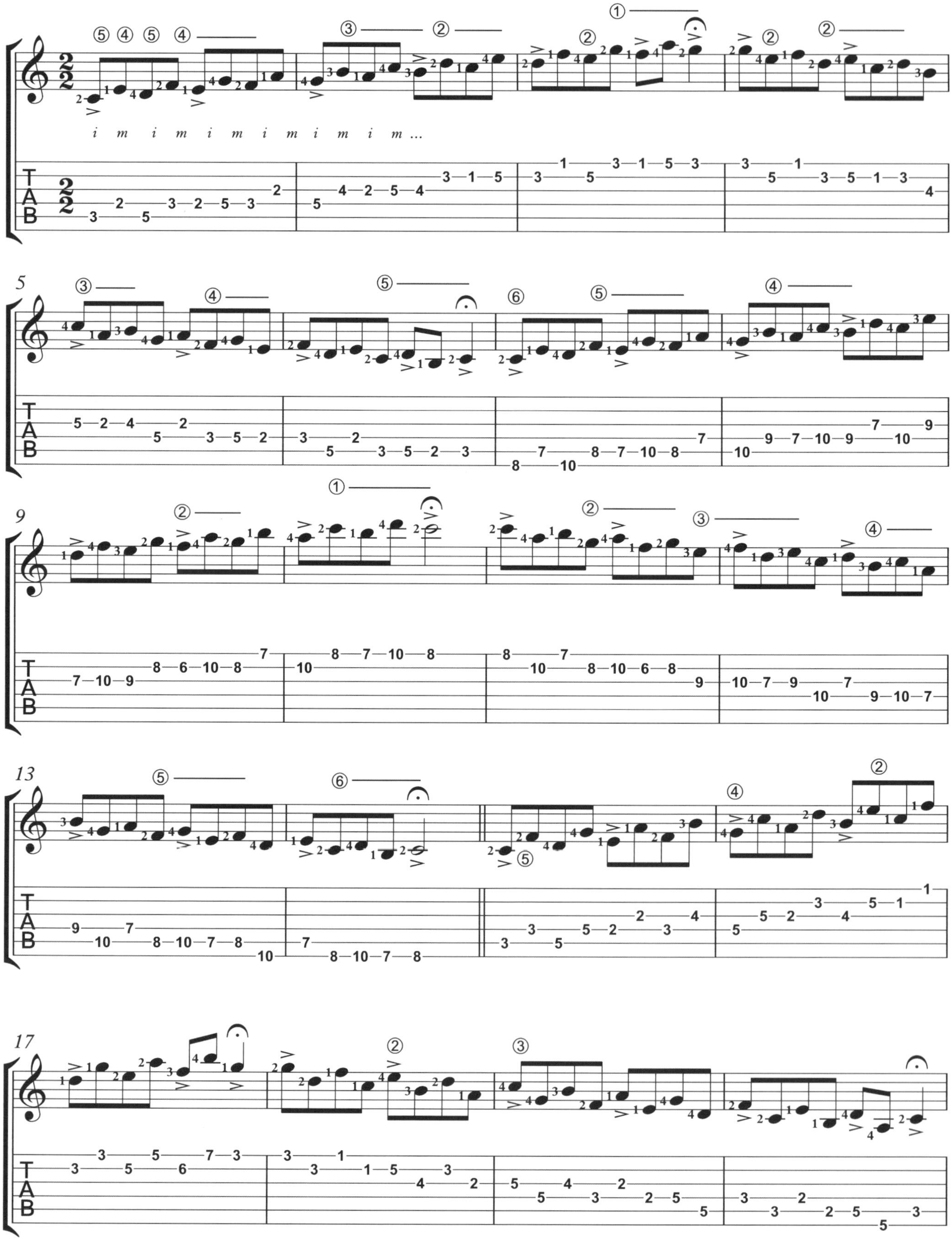
i m i m i m i m i m i m ...
T
A
B
5
9
13
17

21

25

29
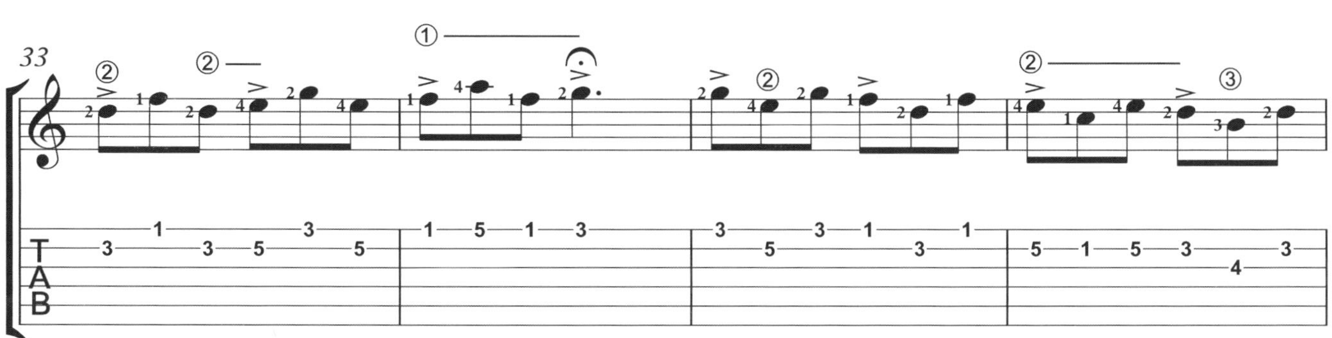
33

37

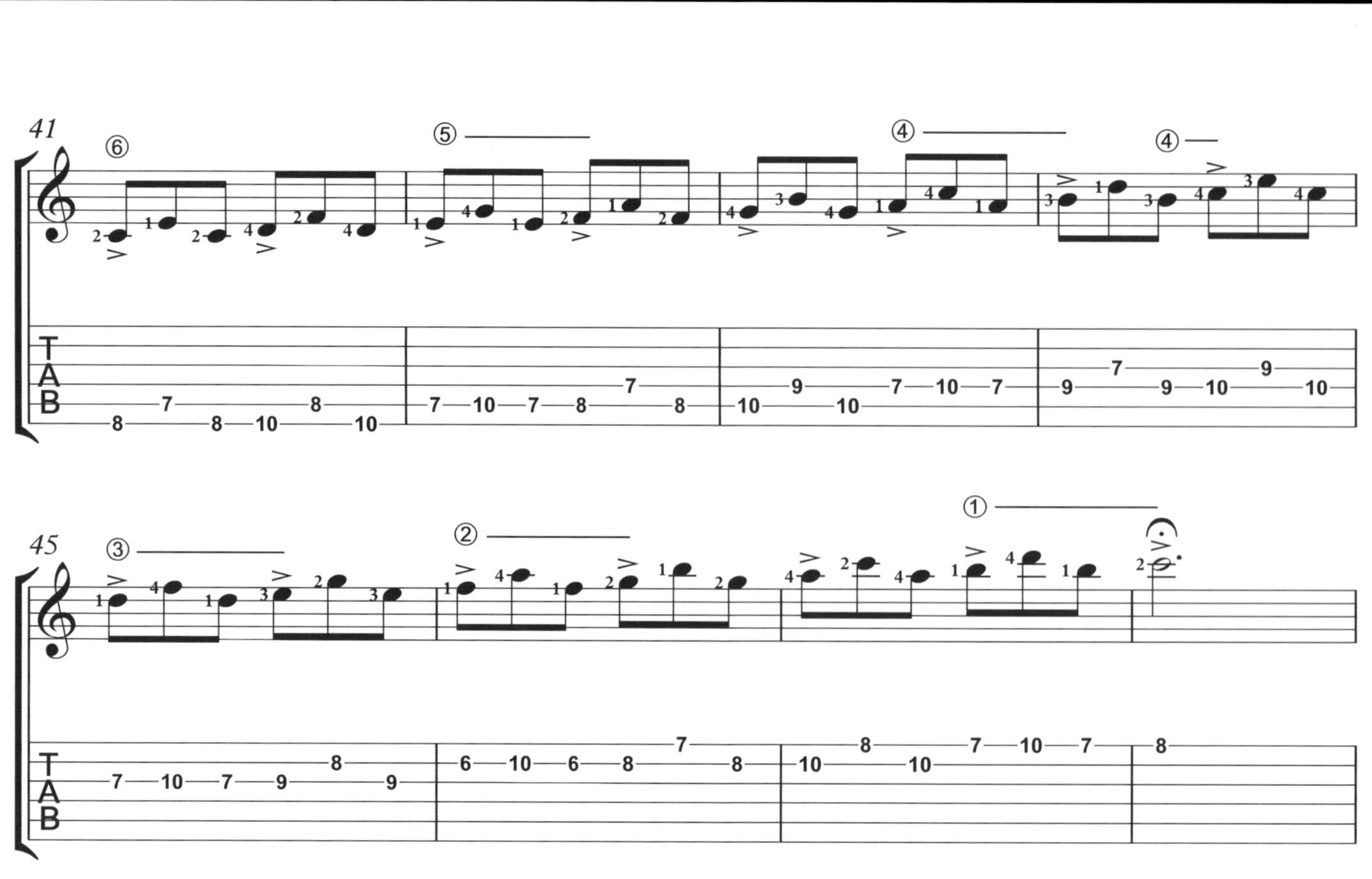
41
T
A
B
45
T
A
B
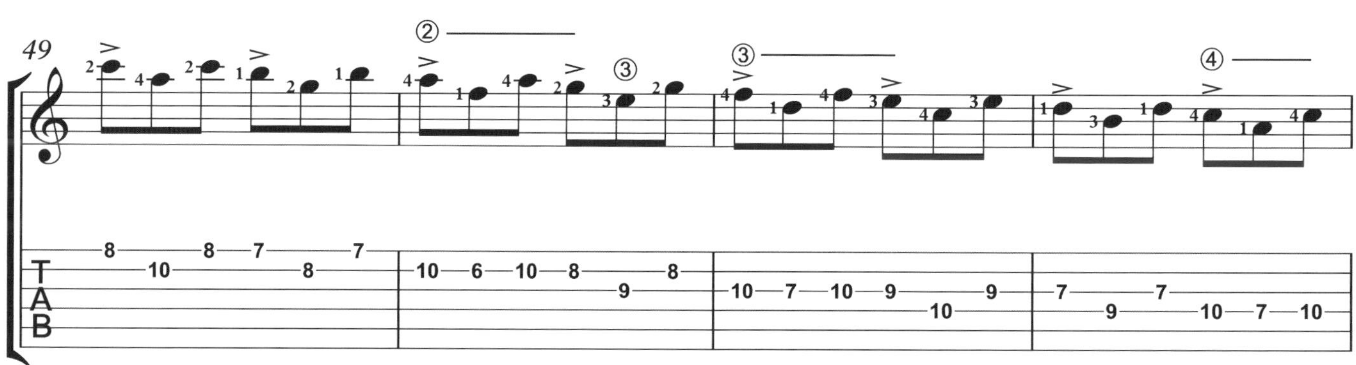
49
T
A
B

53
T
A
B

57
T
A
B

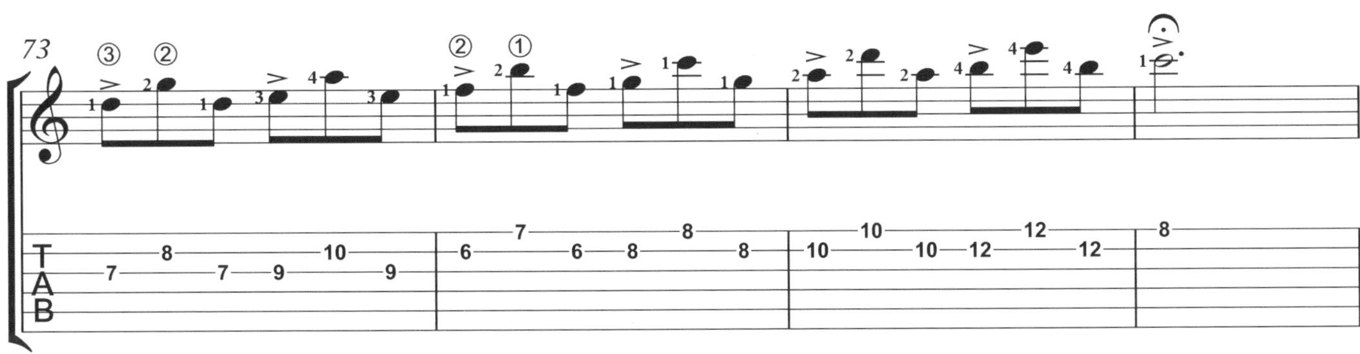
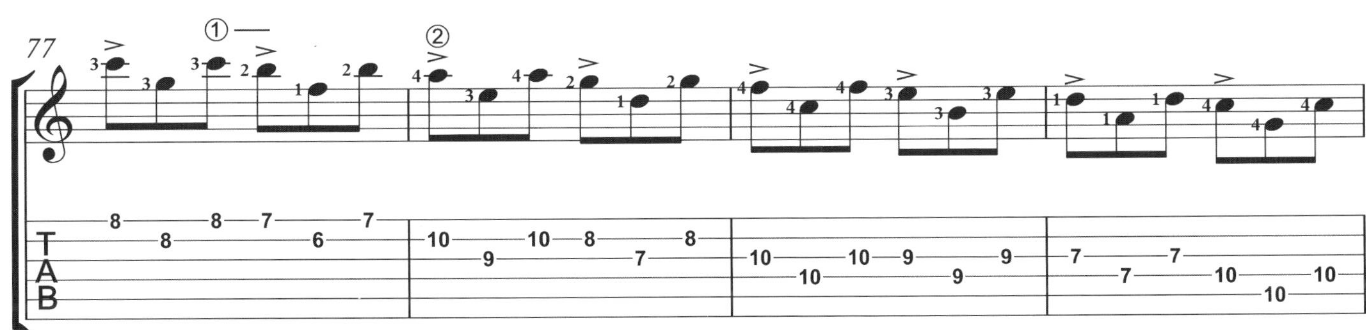

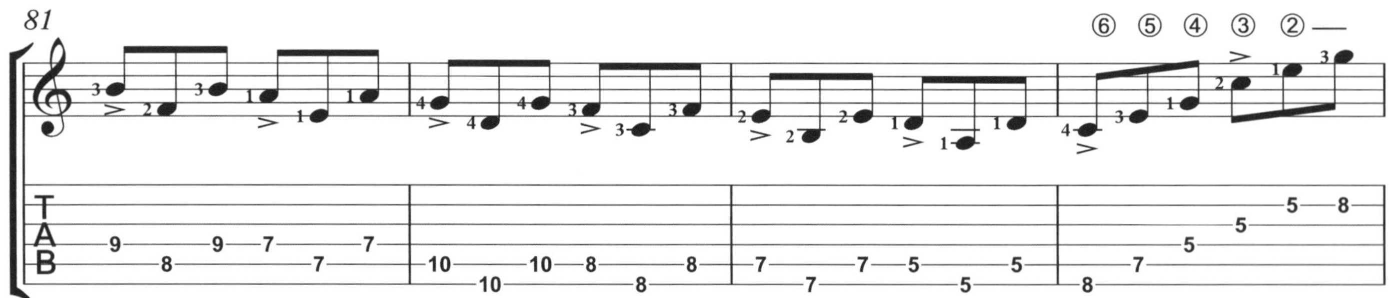
81
⑥ ⑤ ④ ③ ②
T
A
B
9 9 7 7
8 7
10 10 8 8
10 8
7 7 5 5
7 5
5 8
5
5
7
8

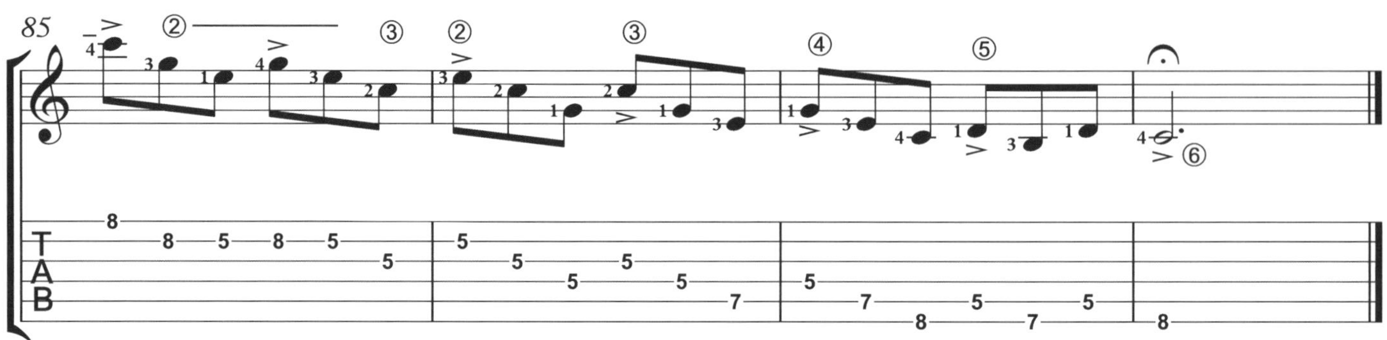
85
② ③
② ③
④ ⑤
⑥
T
A
B
8
8 5 8 5
5
5
5 5
5 5
7
5
7 5 5
8 7
8

ETUDE III

Arpeggio Study

You will practice arpeggio technique in Em.

"The guitar is a golden prison."

Manolo Sanlúcar

Etude III
Chords

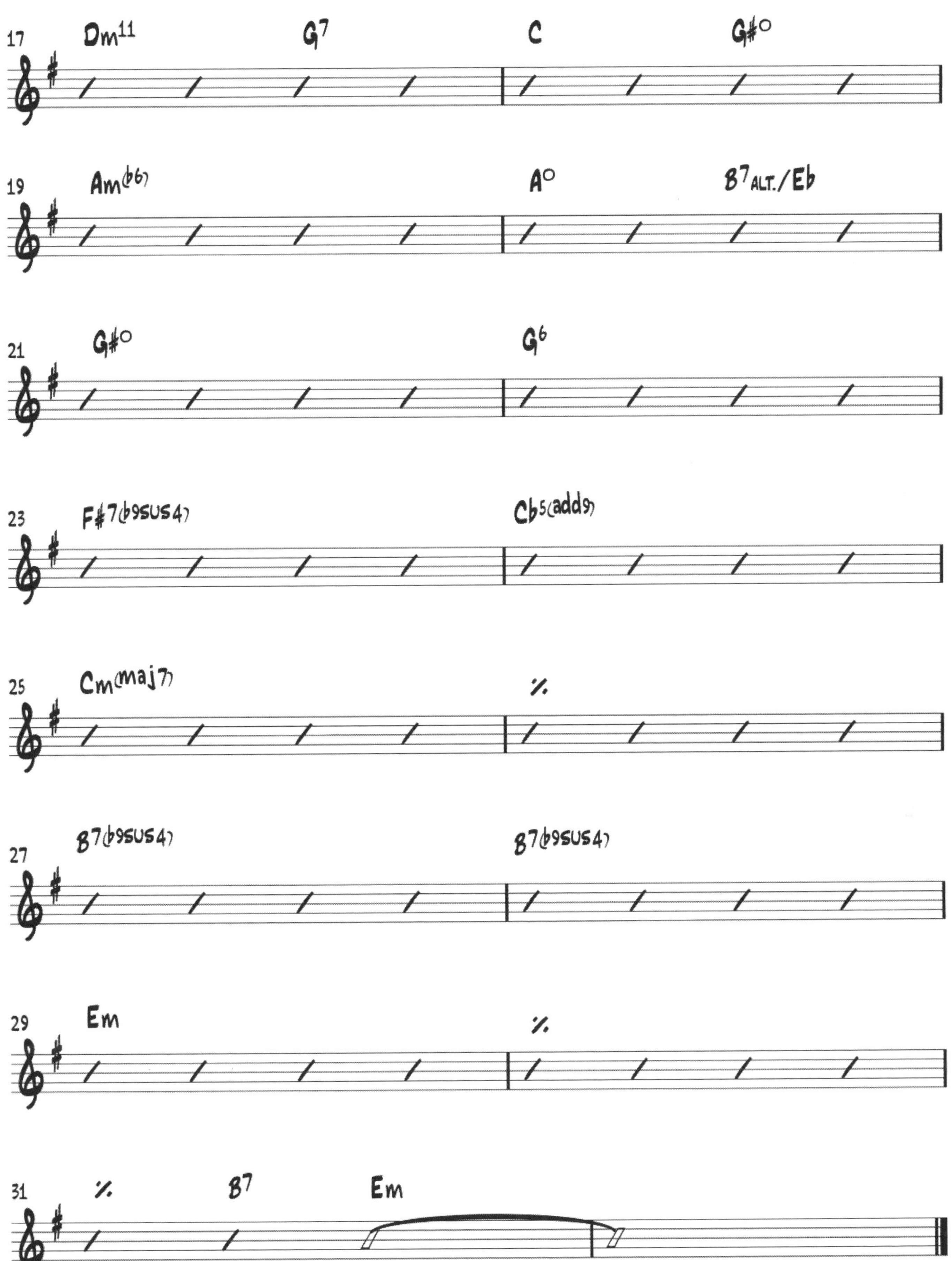
17
Dm11
G7
C
G#o
19
Am(b6)
Ao
B7ALT./Eb
21
G#o
G6
23
F#7(b9SUS4)
Cb5(add9)
25
Cm(maj7)
27
B7(b9SUS4)
B7(b9SUS4)
29
Em
31
B7
Em

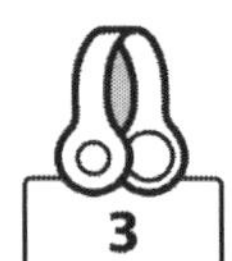

Etude III

Tempo primo ♩=*140*

Music and transcription by
YAGO SANTOS

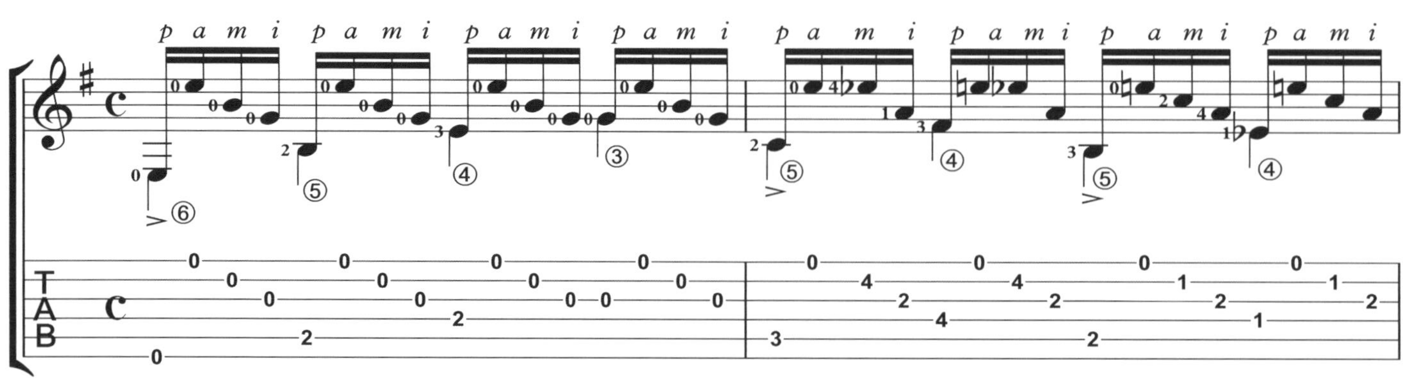

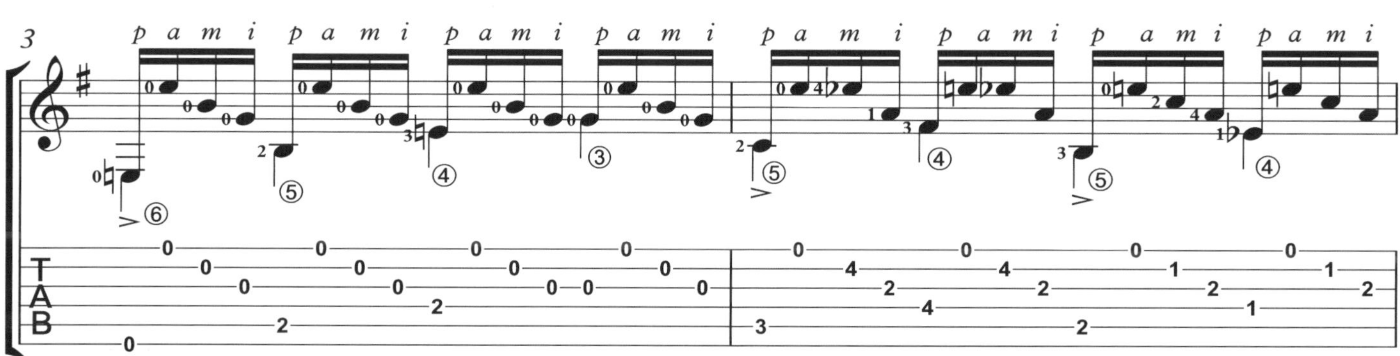

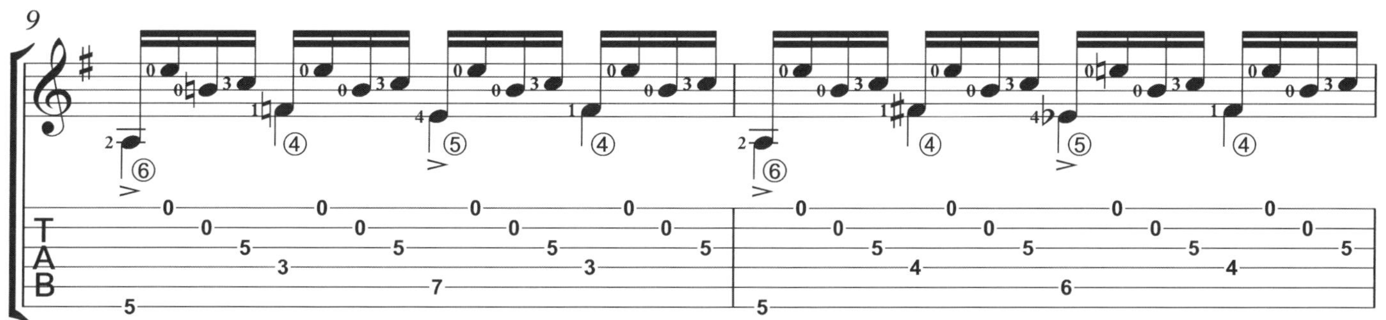
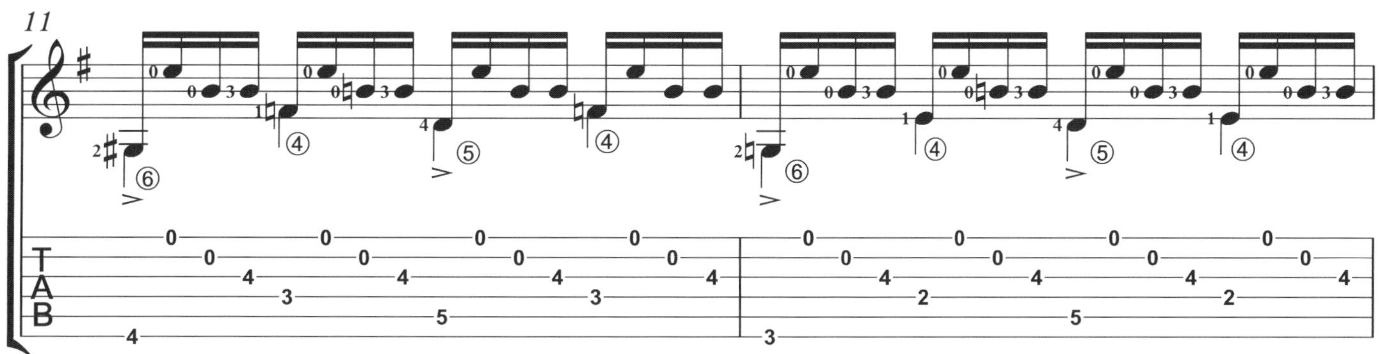
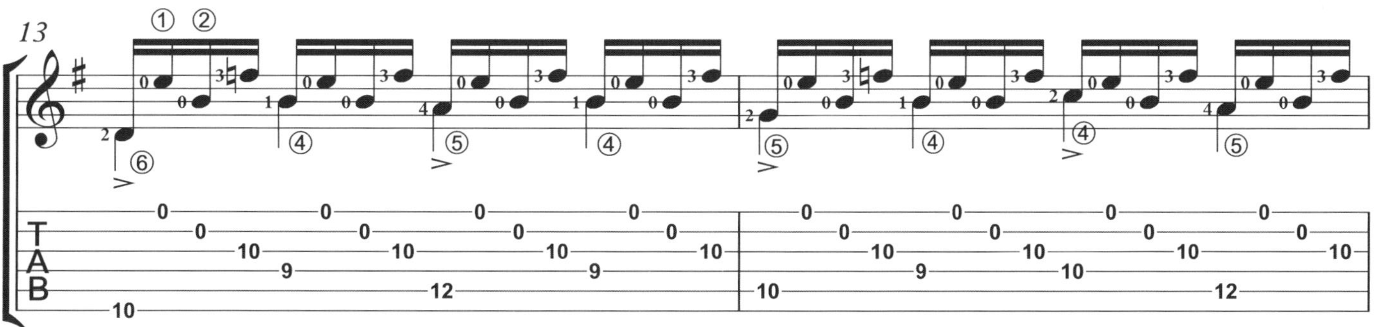
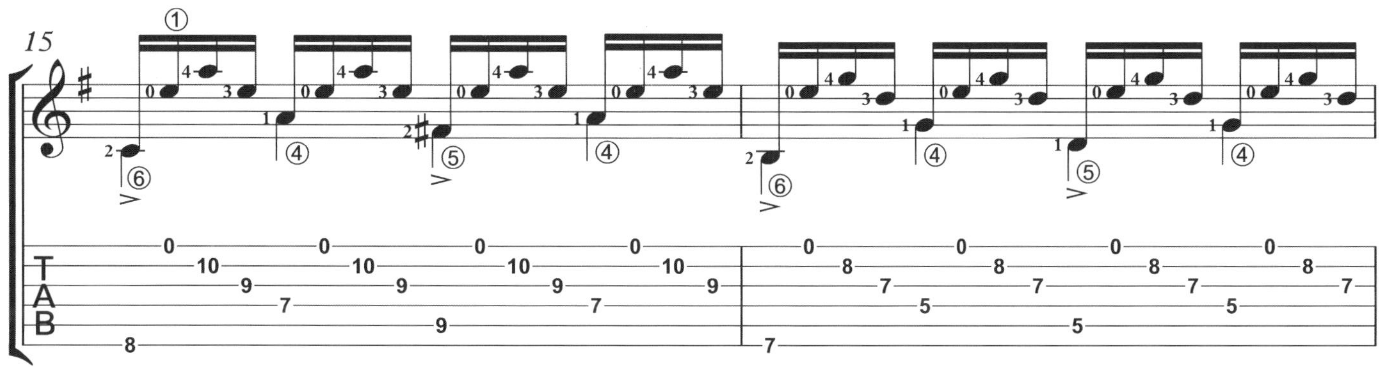
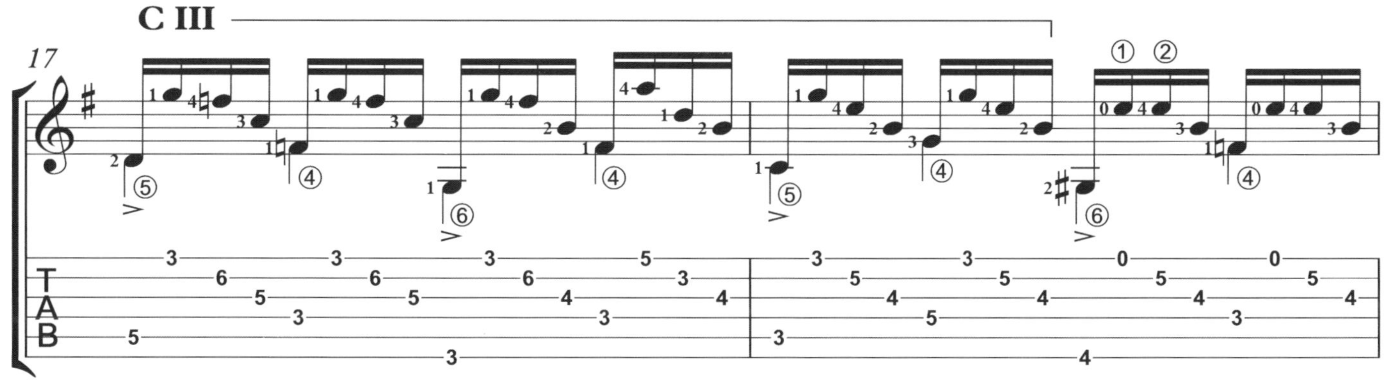
C III

19
T
A
B

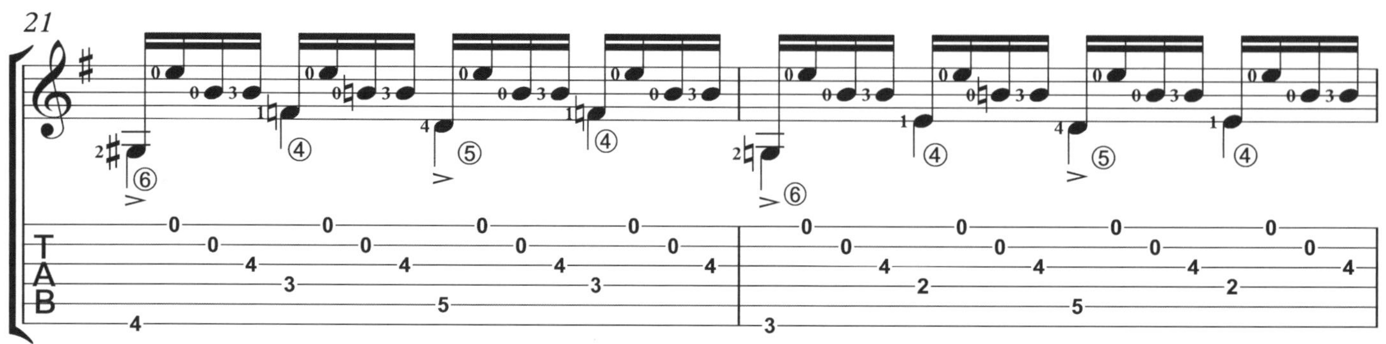
21
T
A
B

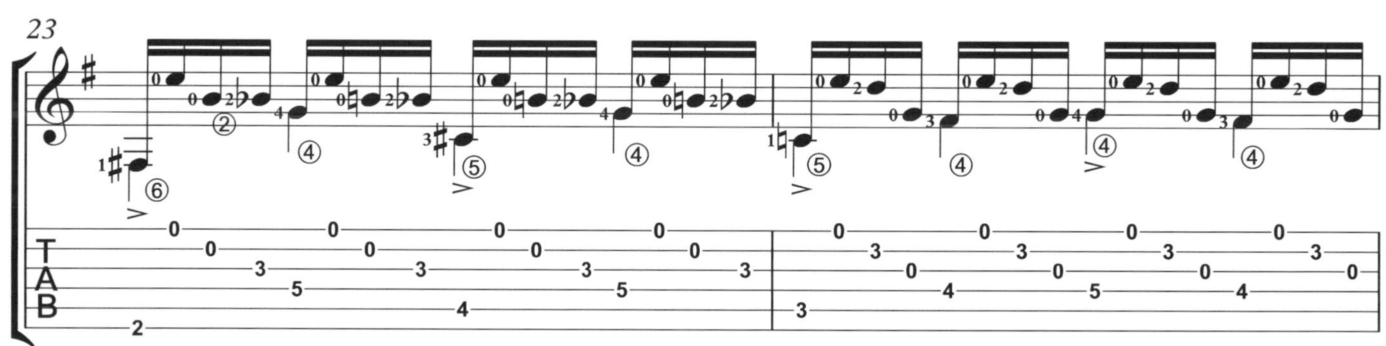
23
T
A
B

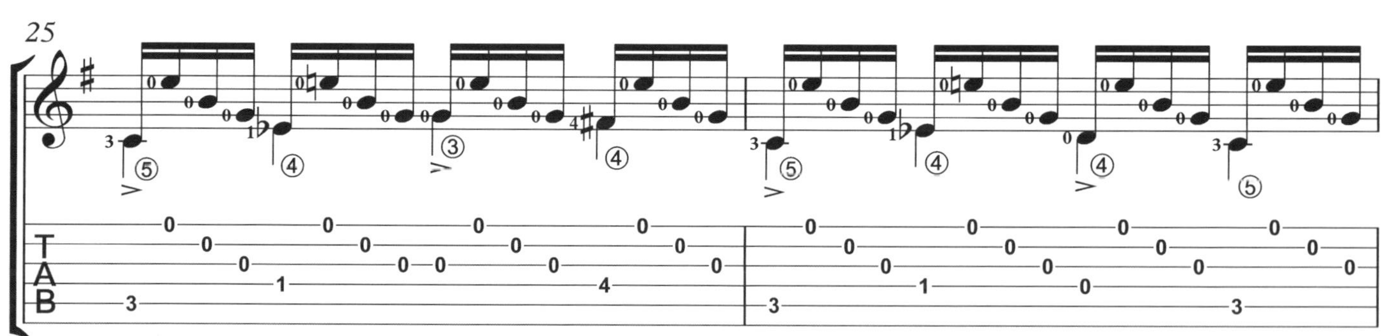
25
T
A
B

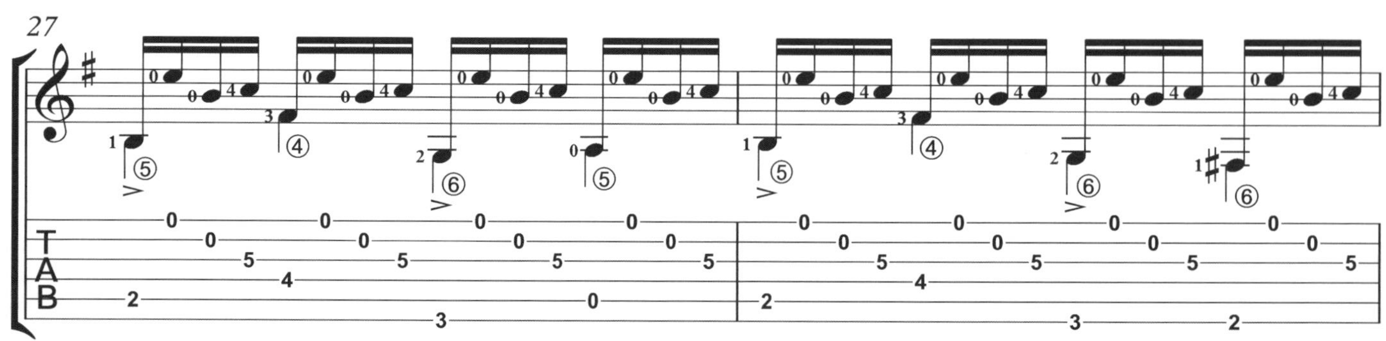
27
T
A
B

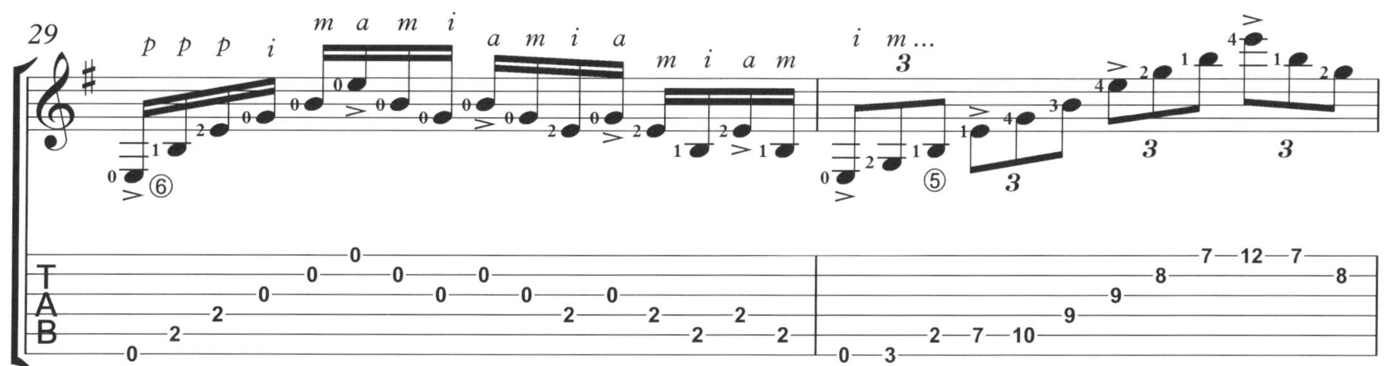
29
p p p i
m a m i
a m i a
m i a m
i m...

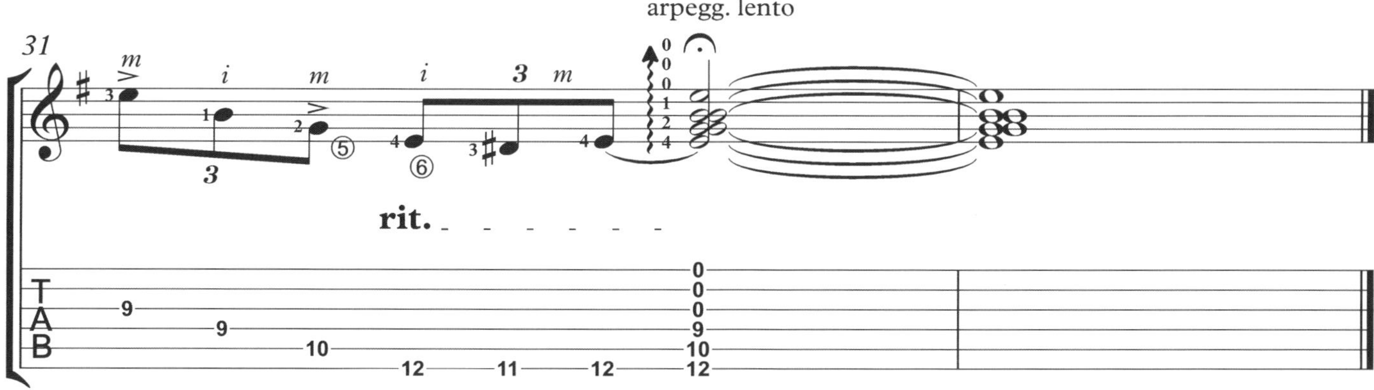
31
arpegg. lento
rit.

ETUDE IV

Interval Study

Now we'll practice alternating intervals of thirds and fourths.

Etude IV

Music and transcription by
YAGO SANTOS

Tempo ♩=*100*

m i m i m i m i m i m i... simile

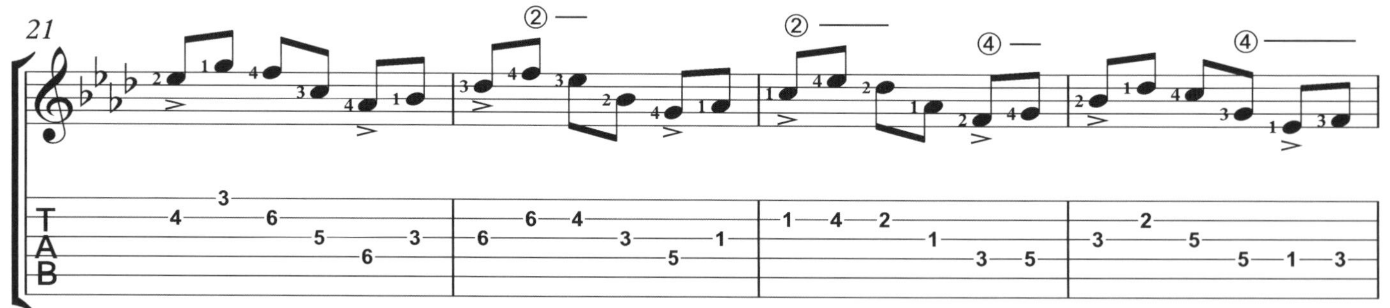
21
②
④
T
A
B

25
③
⑤
④
T
A
B

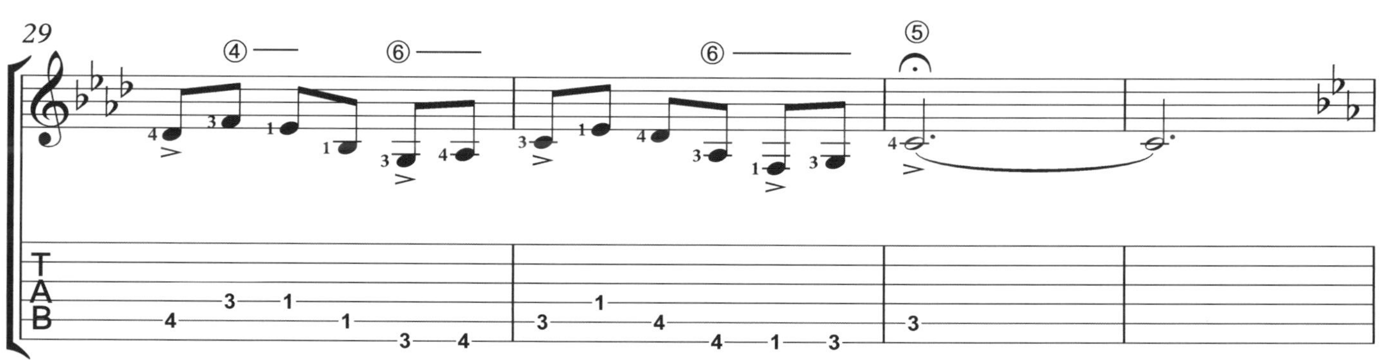
29
④
⑥
⑤
T
A
B

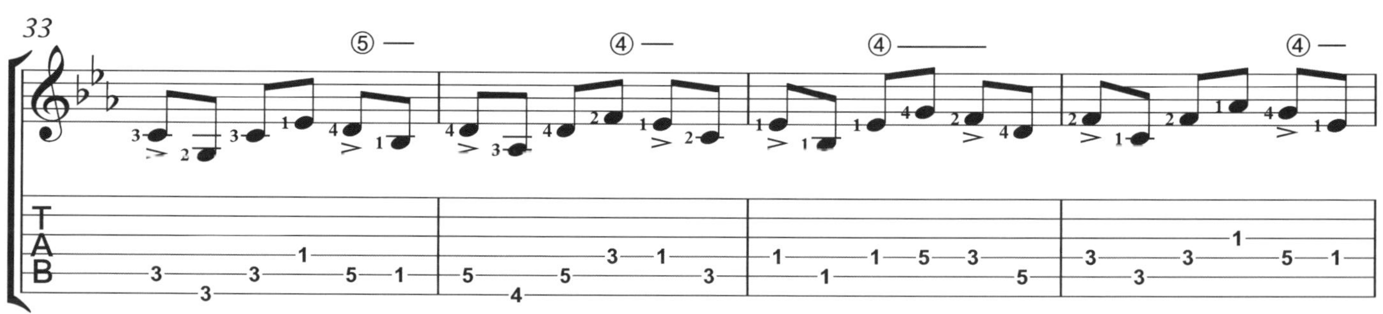
33
⑤
④
T
A
B

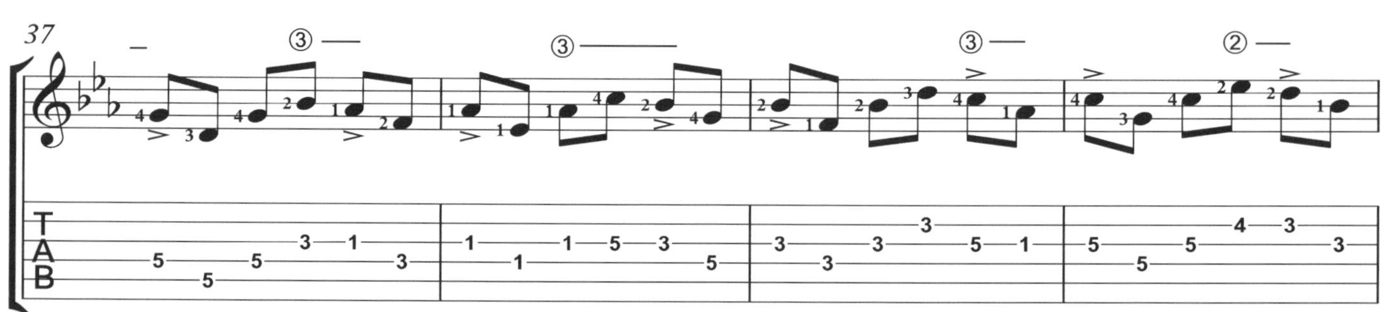
37
③
②
T
A
B

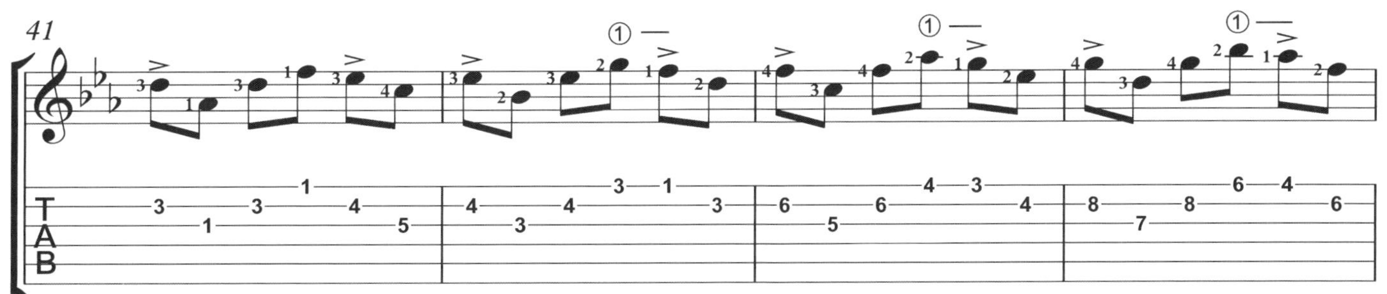
41
T
A
B

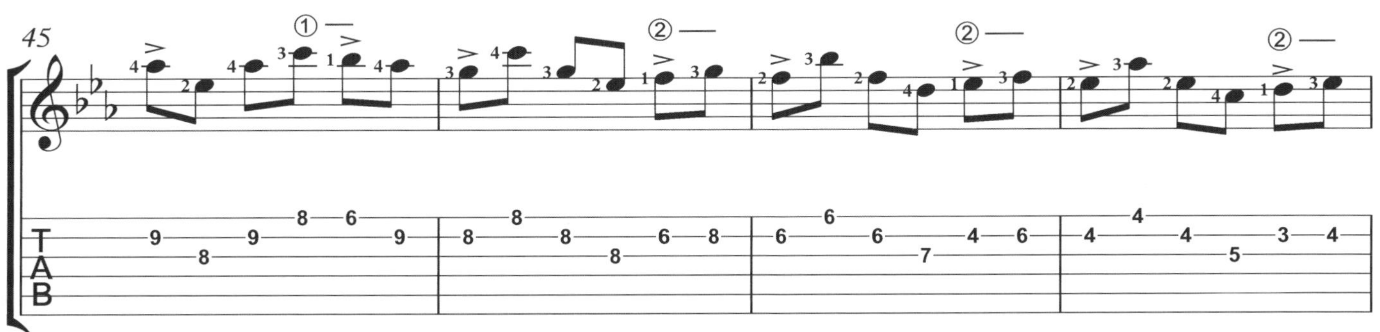
45
T
A
B

49
T
A
B

53
T
A
B

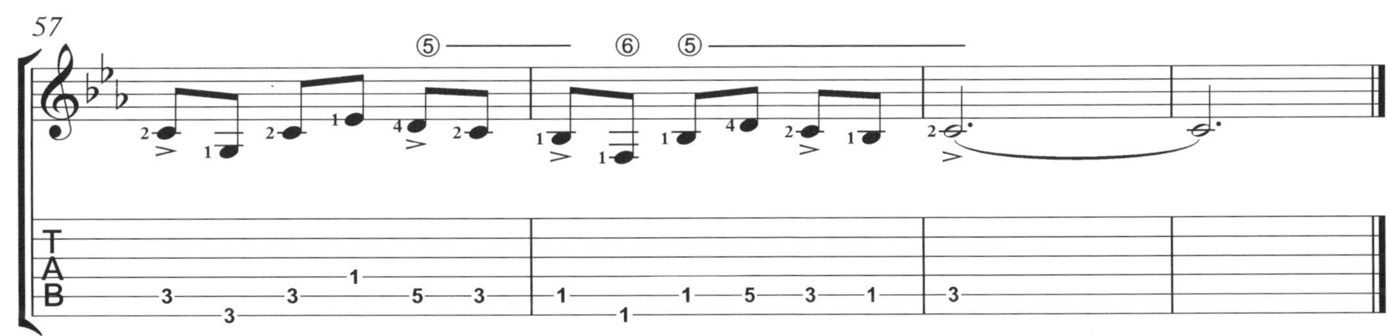
57
T
A
B

ETUDE V

Arpeggio Study

In this etude, you will practice the arpeggio pattern:
p / p / i / a / m / i / a / m / i / a / m / i

"Lean your body slightly forward to support the guitar with your chest and thus the poetry of music resounds in your heart."

Andrés Segovia

Etude V
Chords

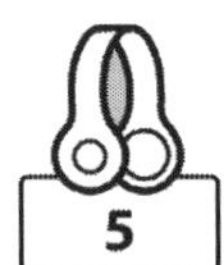

Etude V

Vivace ♩=115

Music and transcription by
YAGO SANTOS

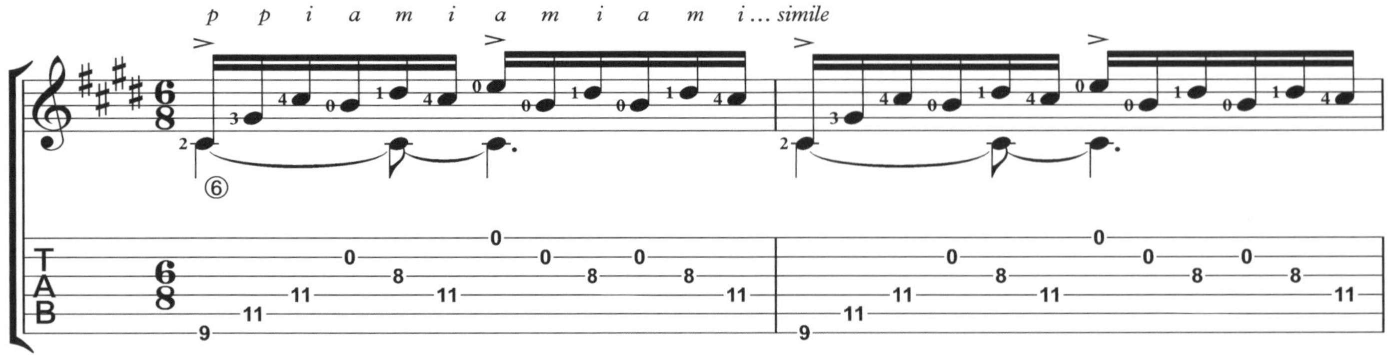

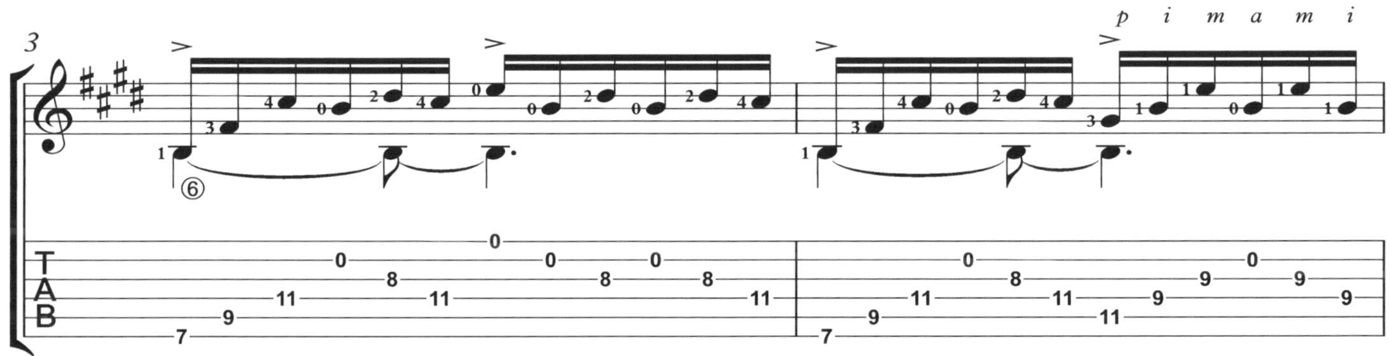

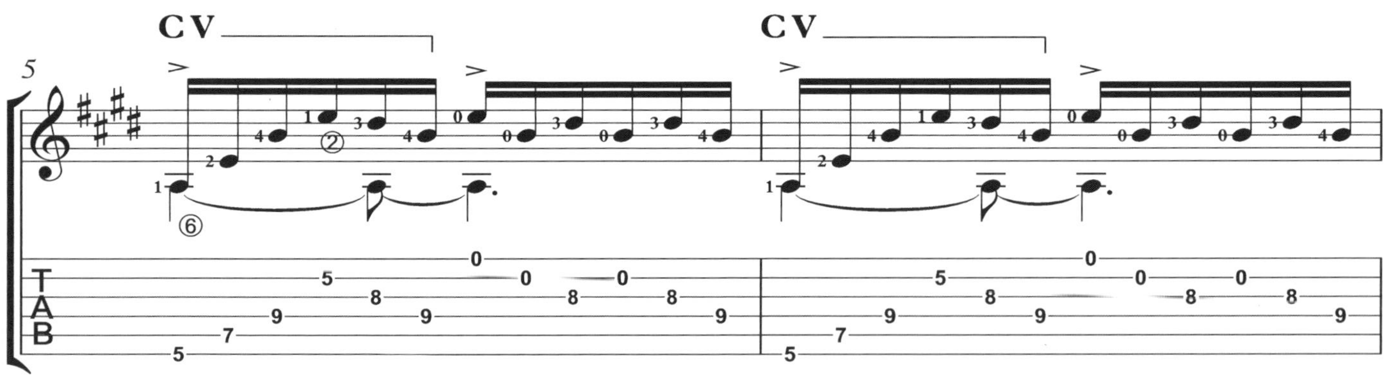

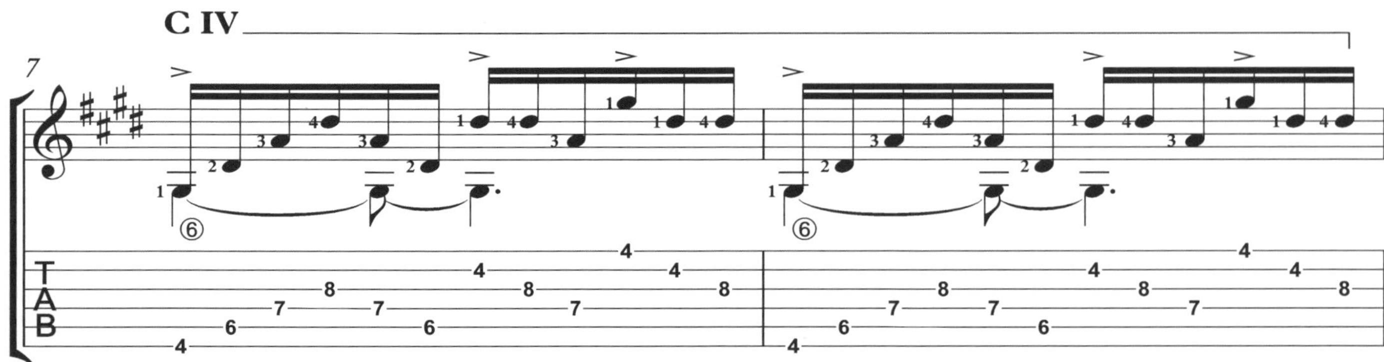

p i m a m i a m i a m i ... sigue
C VII
C IV
T
A
B

arpegg. lento

ETUDE VI

Arpeggio Study

Next, you'll practice left-hand arpeggio technique to improve your phrasing for improvising and composing.

"If you pick up a guitar and it says, 'Take me, I'm yours,' then that's the guitar for you."

Frank Zappa

Etude VI
Chords

YAGO SANTOS

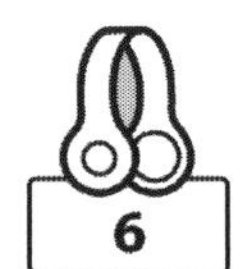

Etude VI

Moderato ♩*=110*

Music and transcription by
YAGO SANTOS

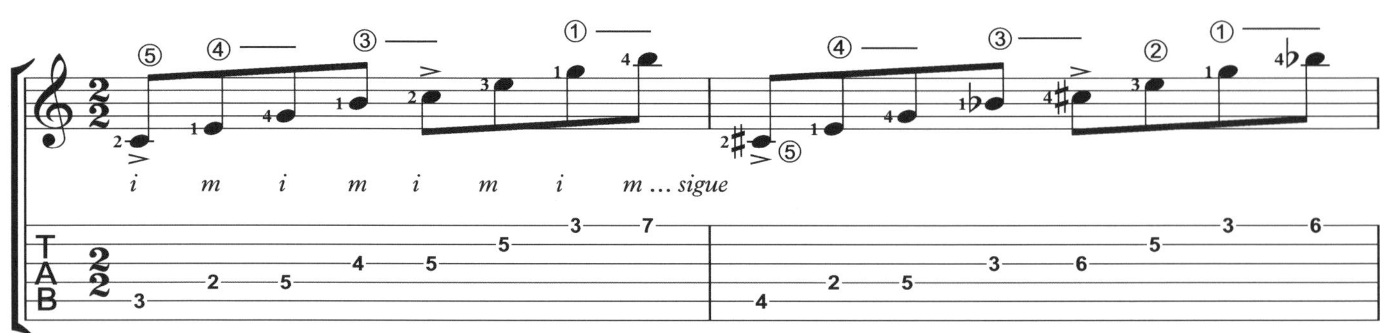

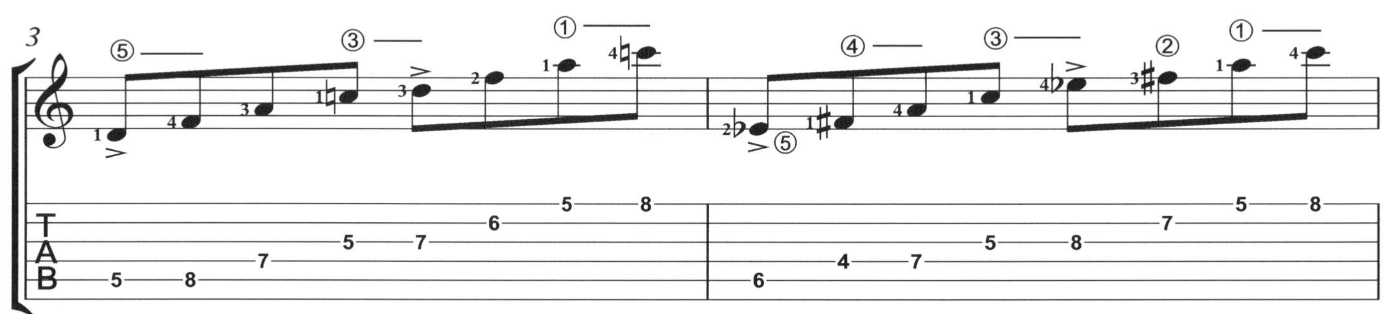

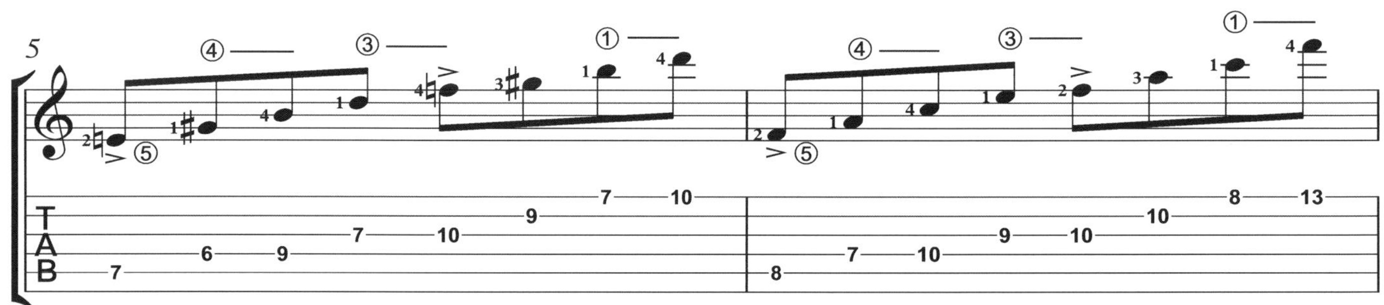

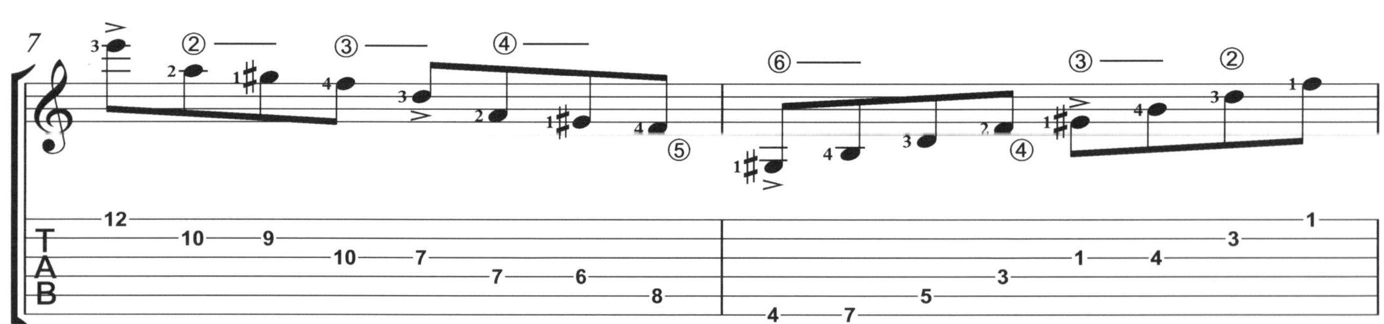

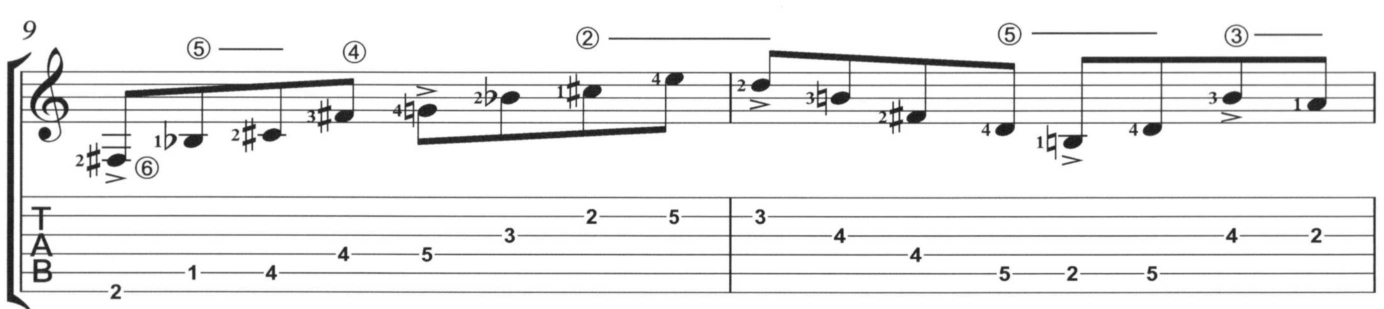

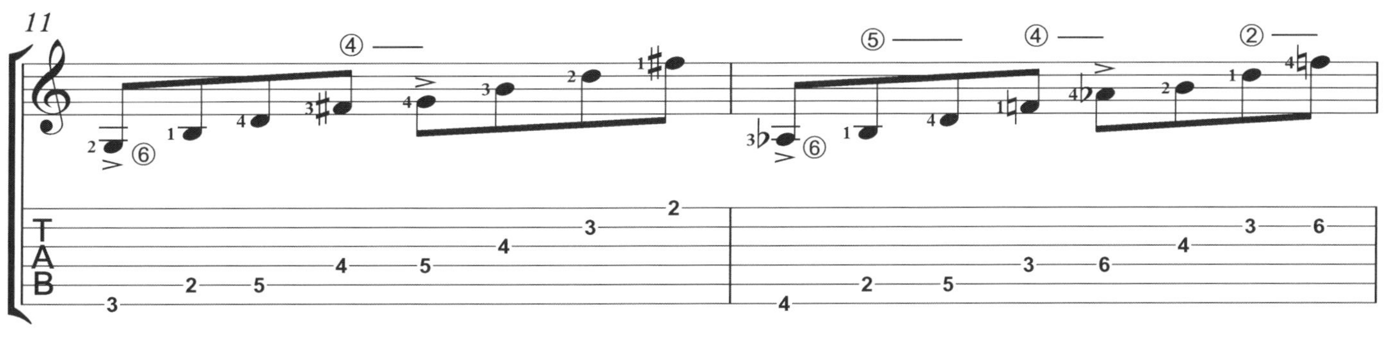
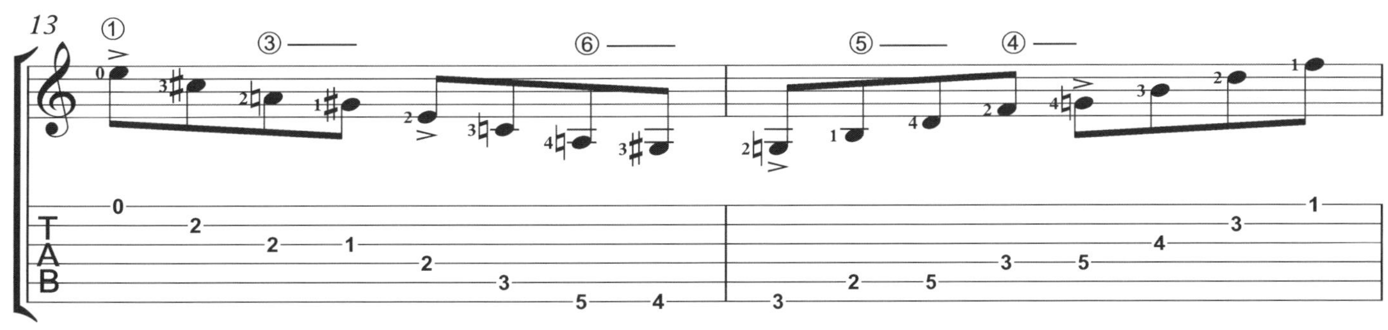
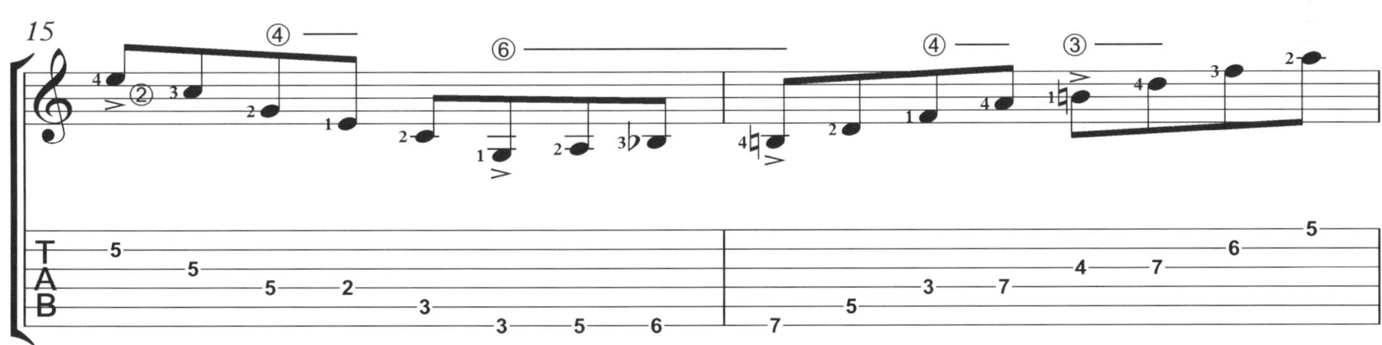
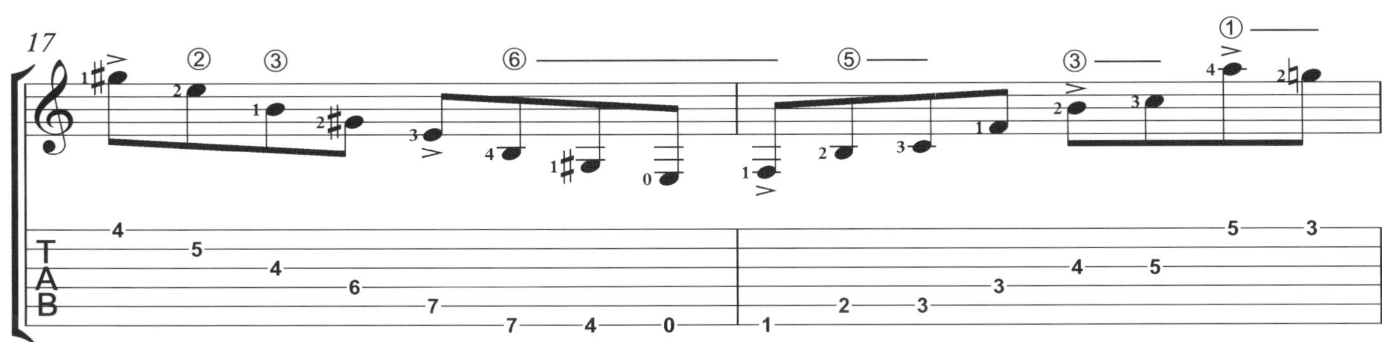
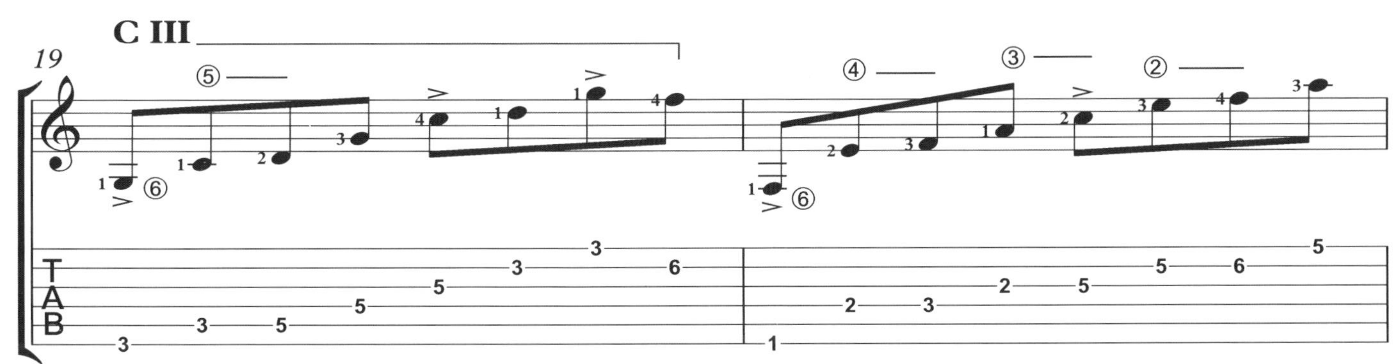
C III

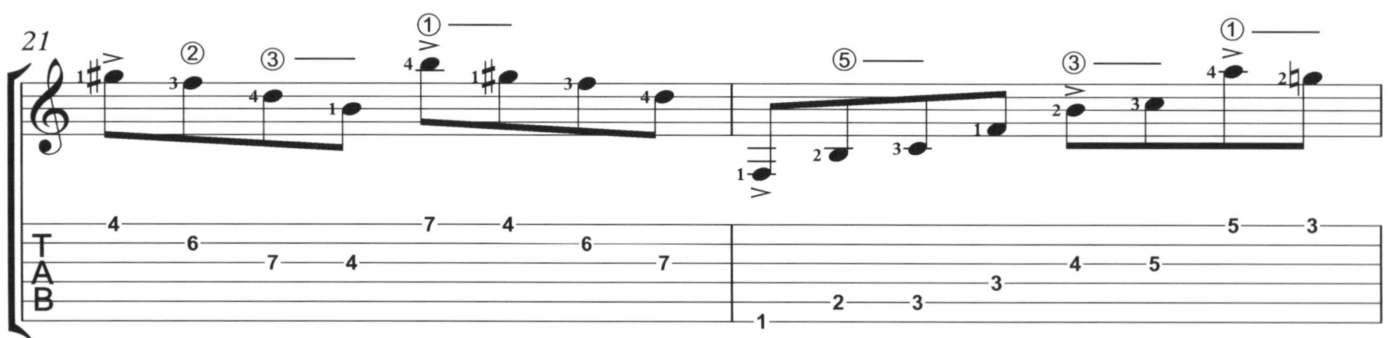

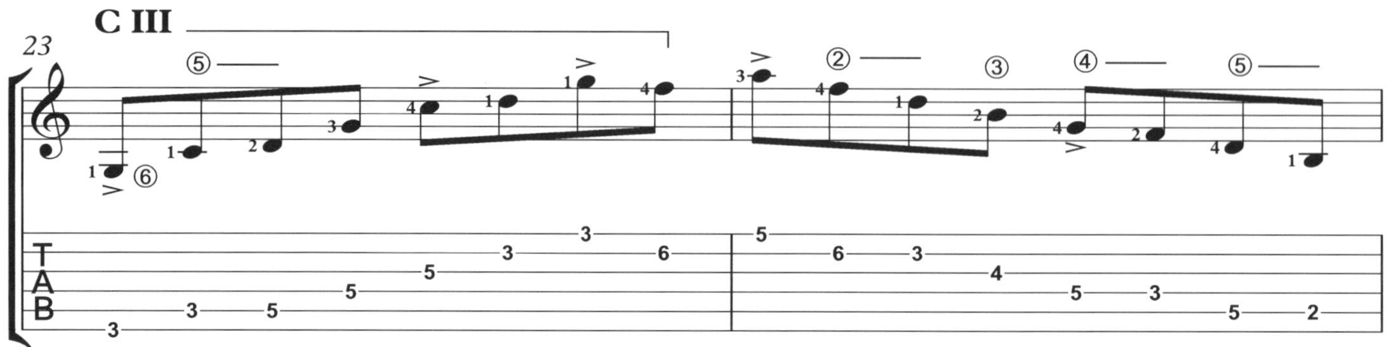
C III

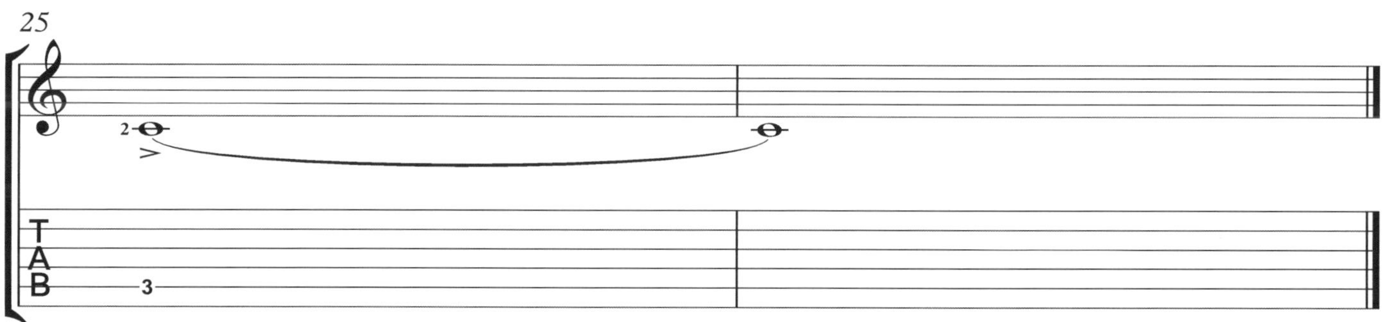

ETUDE VII

Interval Study

In this study, you will practice major sixth and perfect fourth intervals, starting on the eighth fret of the sixth string with the second finger.

Etude VII

Tempo ♩=115

Music and transcription by
YAGO SANTOS

ETUDE VIII

Warm-Up Study

Here, we'll practice picado or rest-stroke technique using *m* / *i* and *p* / *i* in C Ionian or C major.

"Every July, August and part of September I escape from the guitar;
I escape from Paco de Lucía and go to the Caribbean part of Mexico.
I have a little house there where I spend two months listening to music,
without playing because I don't have a guitar with me,
fishing and cooking, and recharging
my batteries for new concerts".

Paco de Lucía

Etude VIII
Chords

Etude VIII

Music and transcription by
YAGO SANTOS

Moderato ♩=*80*

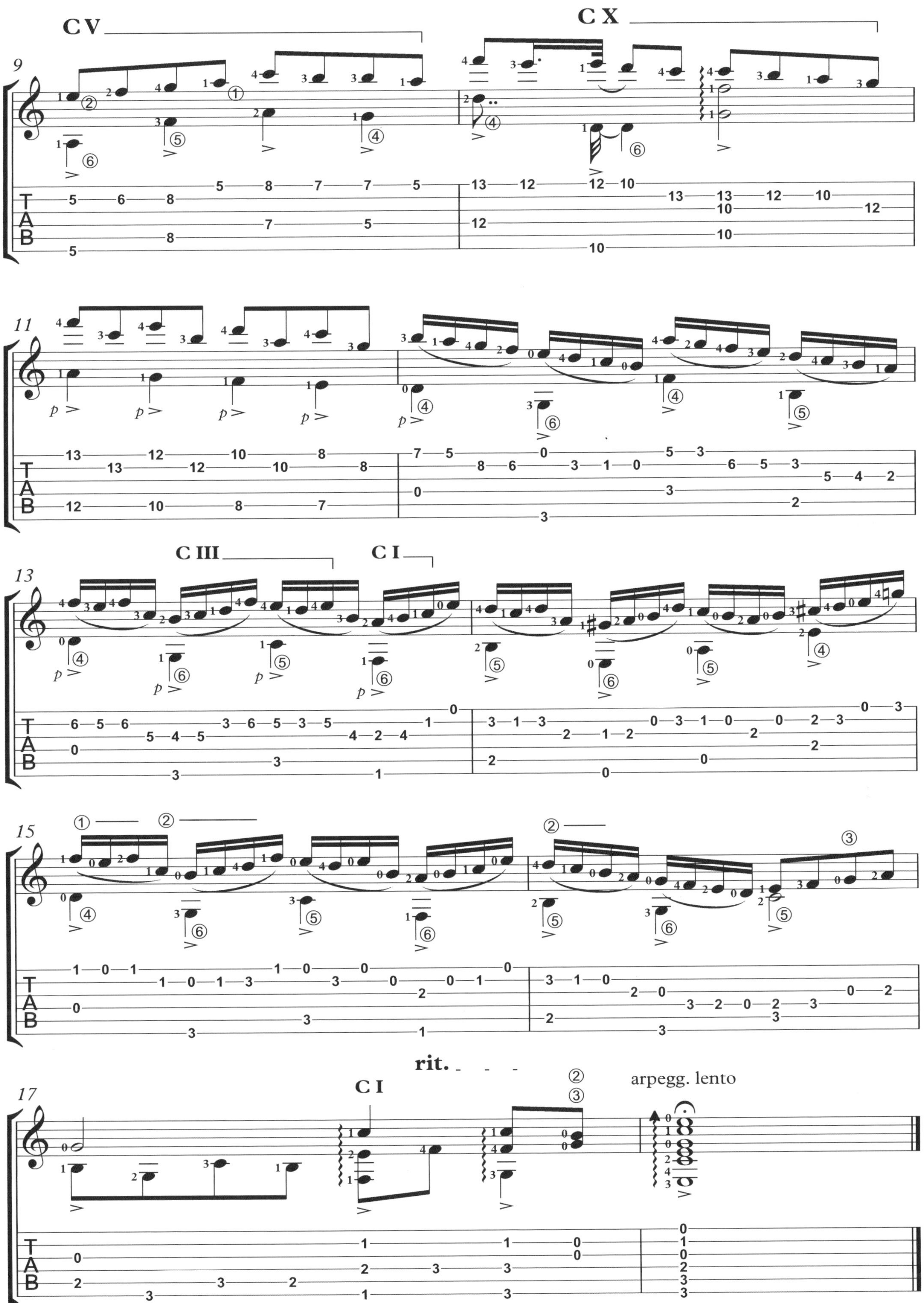
CV
CX
rit.
CIII
CI
arpegg. lento

ETUDE IX

Arpeggio-Ligado Study

This motoric study requires practice with arpeggio-ligado and double-arpeggio technique; it is played with a long *pimiapimiami* pattern in 6/8 time. The pattern varies slightly to accomodate the melody.

"The beauty of learning is that nobody can take it away from you."

B.B. King

Etude IX
Chords

Etude IX

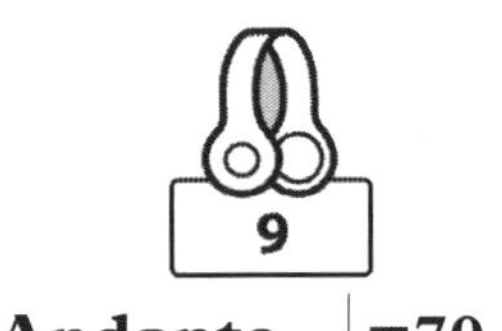

Andante ♩.=70

Music and transcription by
YAGO SANTOS

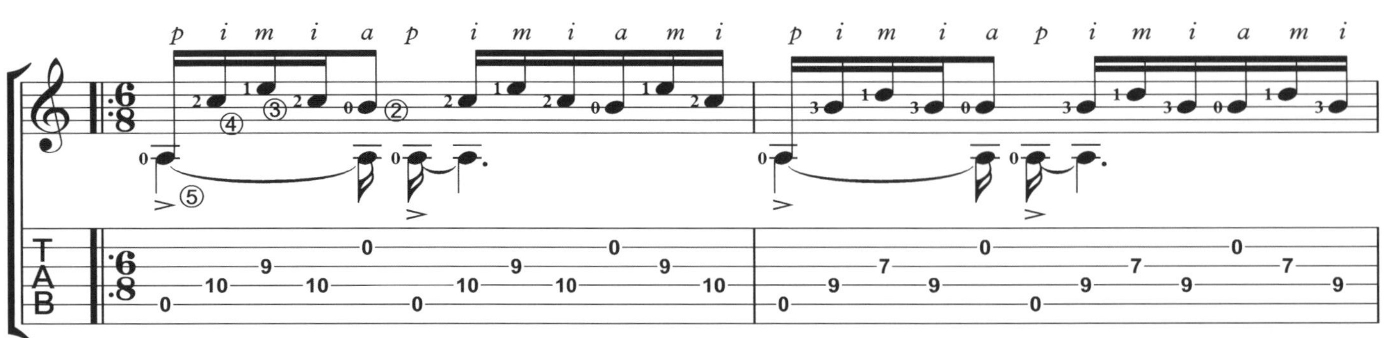

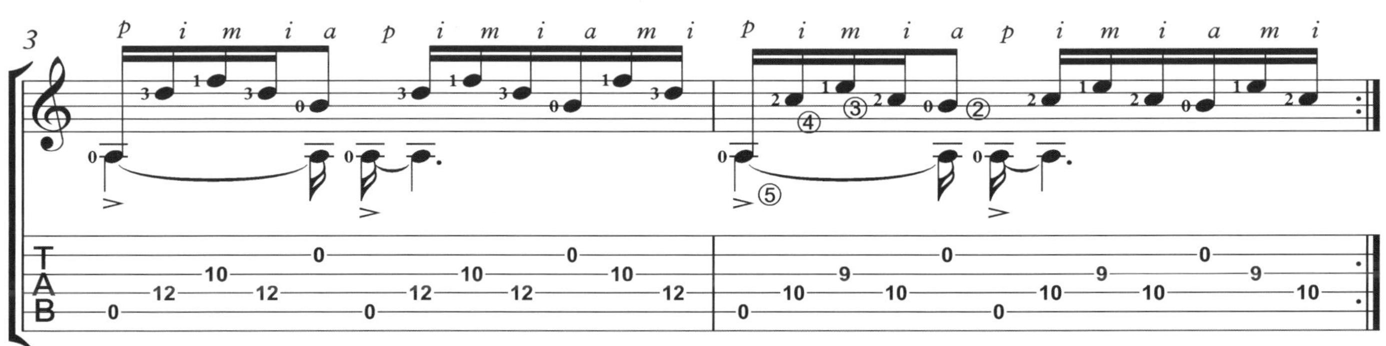

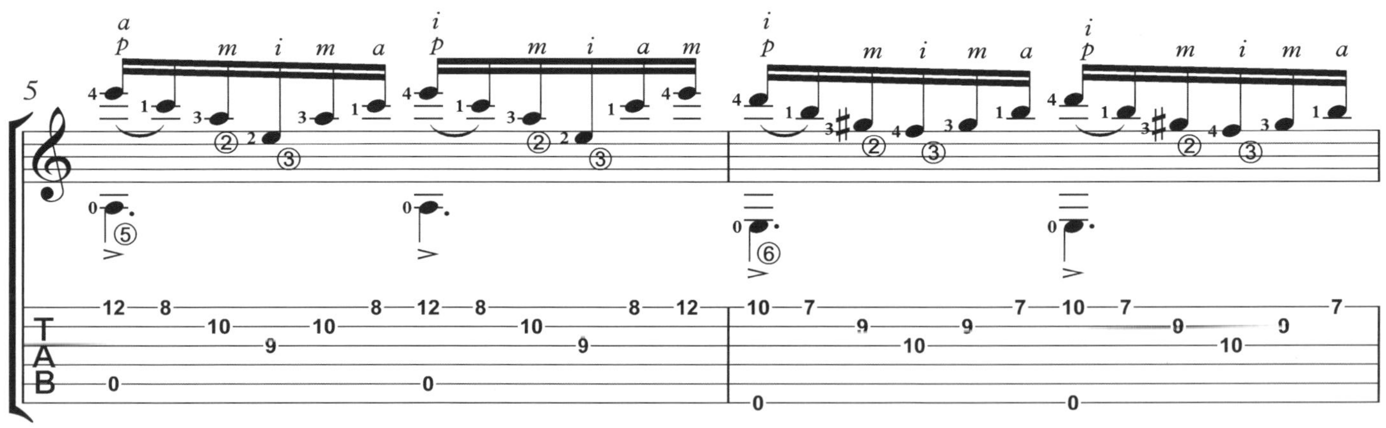

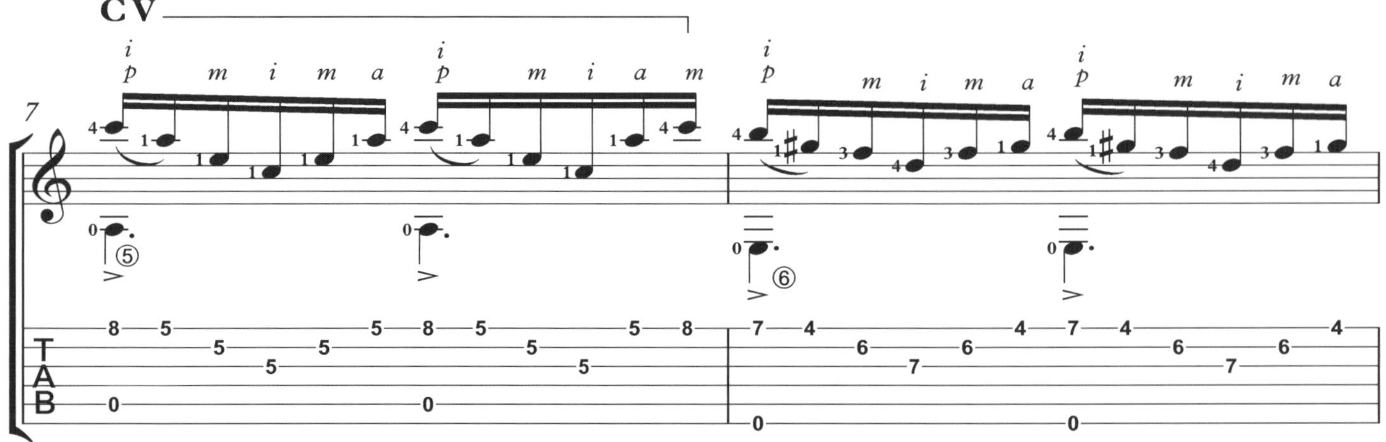

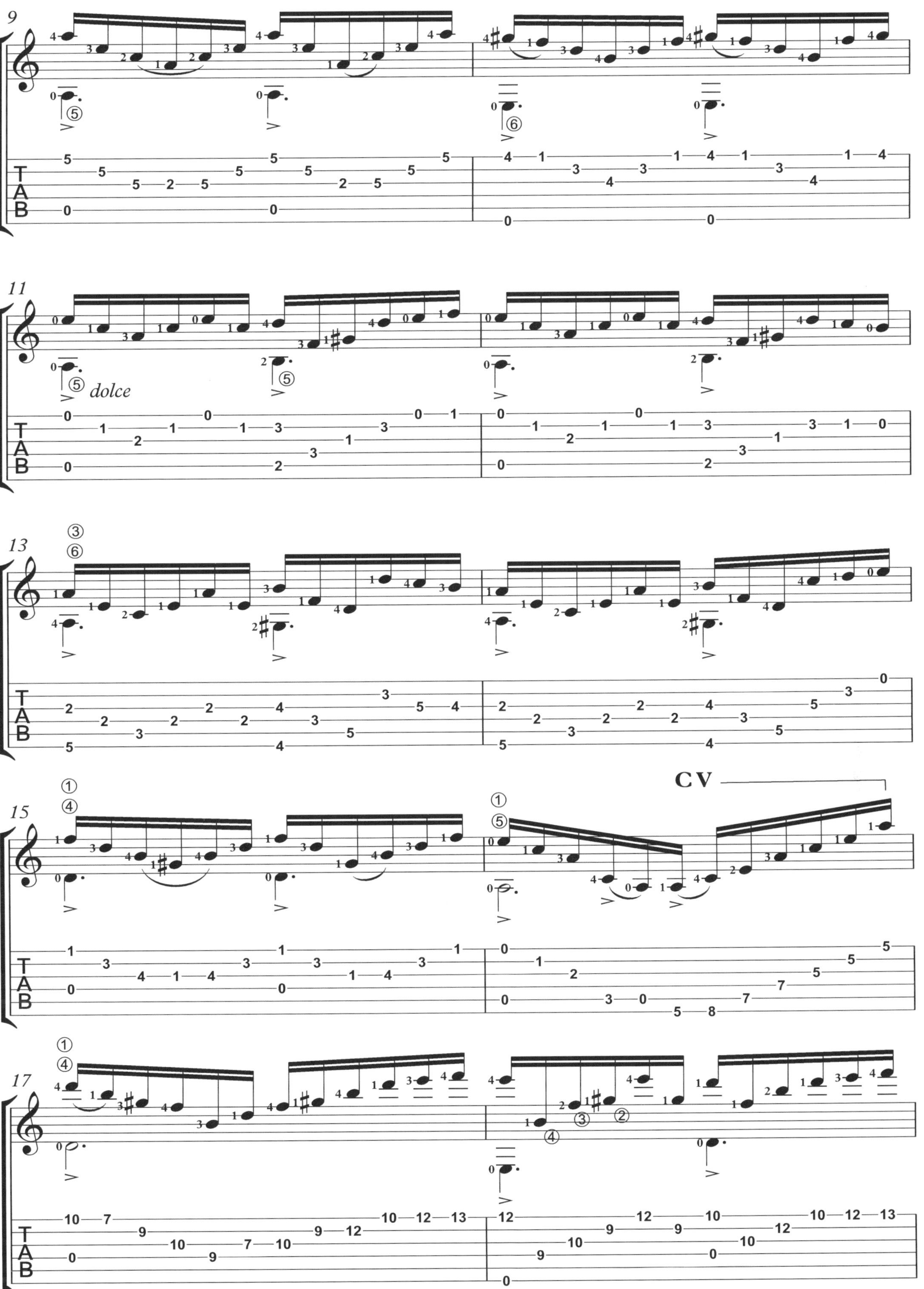
dolce
CV

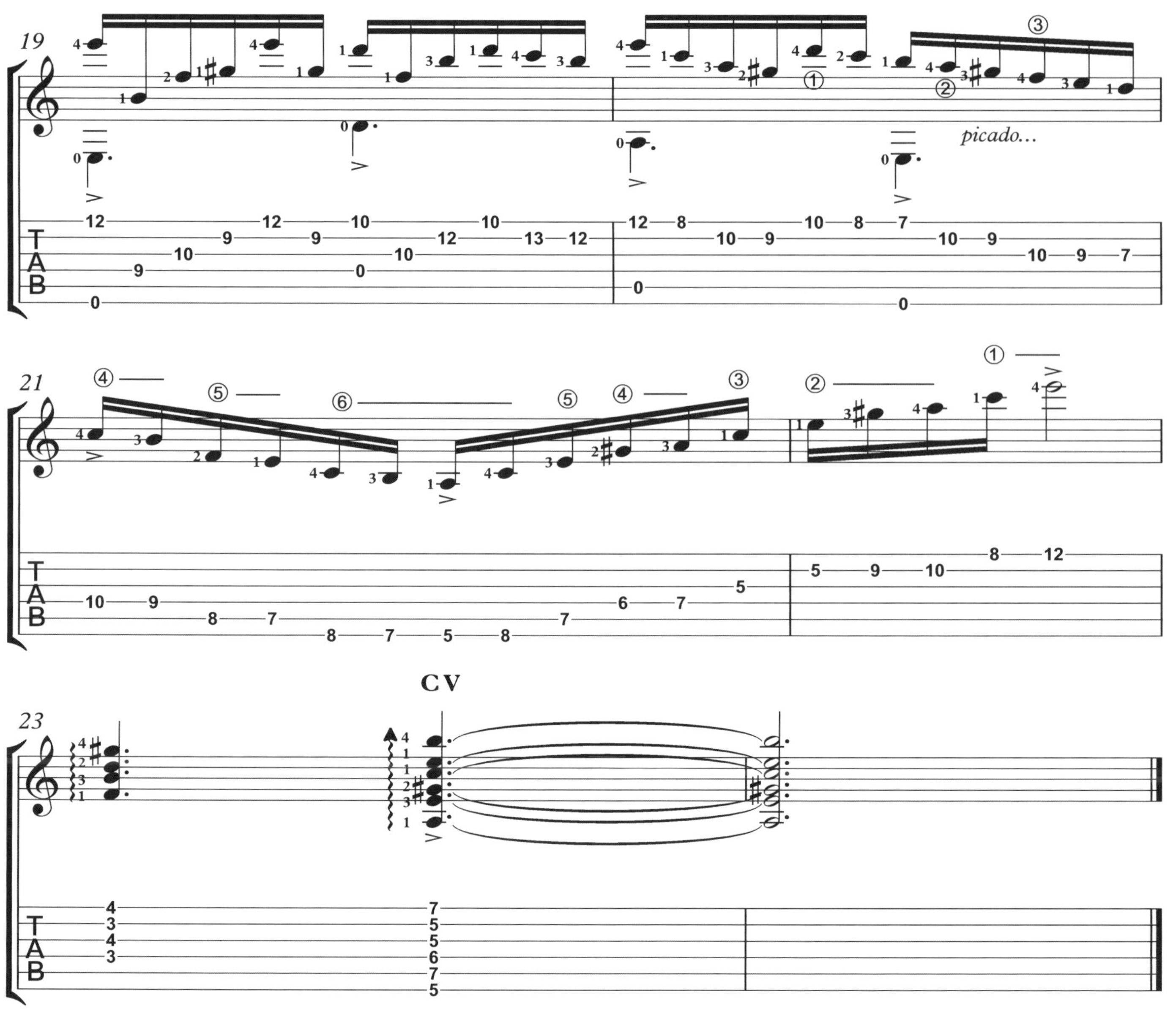
19
picado...
21
23
CV

ETUDE X

Study in Em

This piece offers the opportunity to practice the techniques of picado, ligado and arpeggio, as well as a chance to improve your expressiveness in melodic and harmonic accompaniment.

"Let the guitar be an extension of yourself. Speak with the guitar, communicate with the guitar, say things with the guitar without thinking where you are going and then investigate and look for ideas; to get to this point you have to spend many hours with the guitar."

Rafael Riqueni

Etude X
Chords

Etude X

Music and transcription by
YAGO SANTOS

A tempo ♩.=55

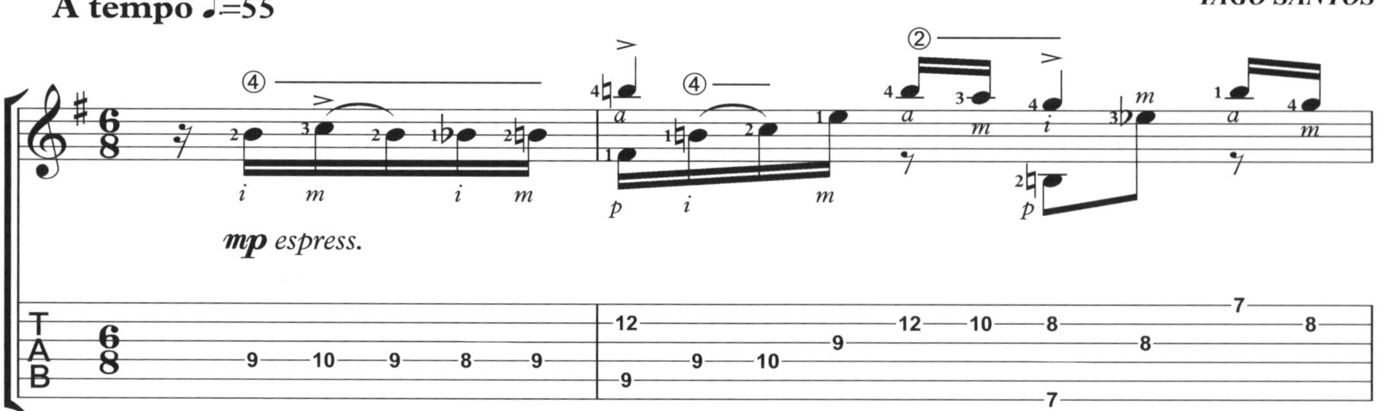

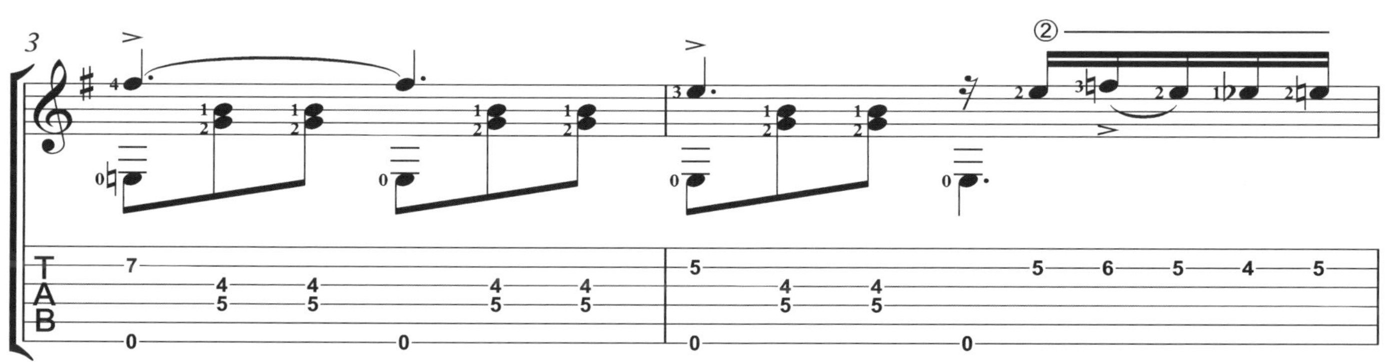

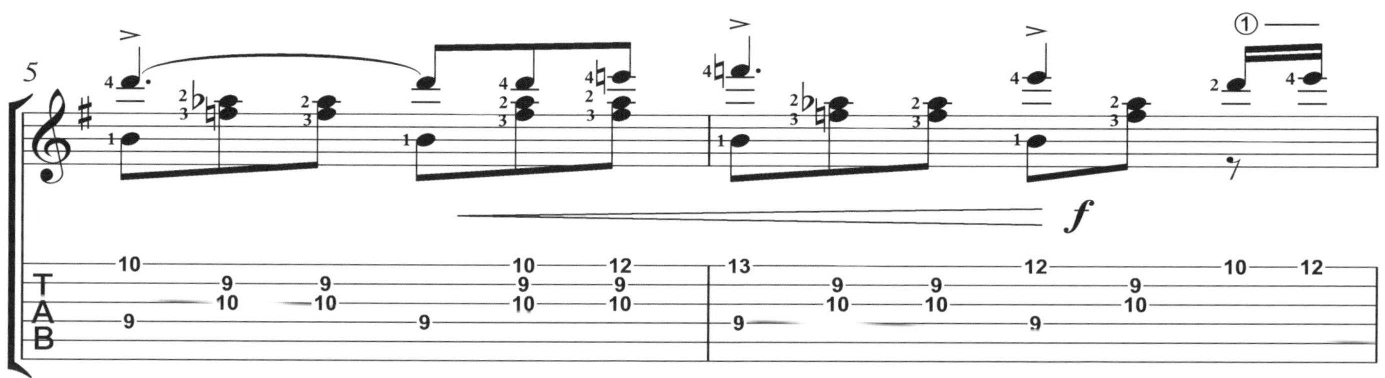

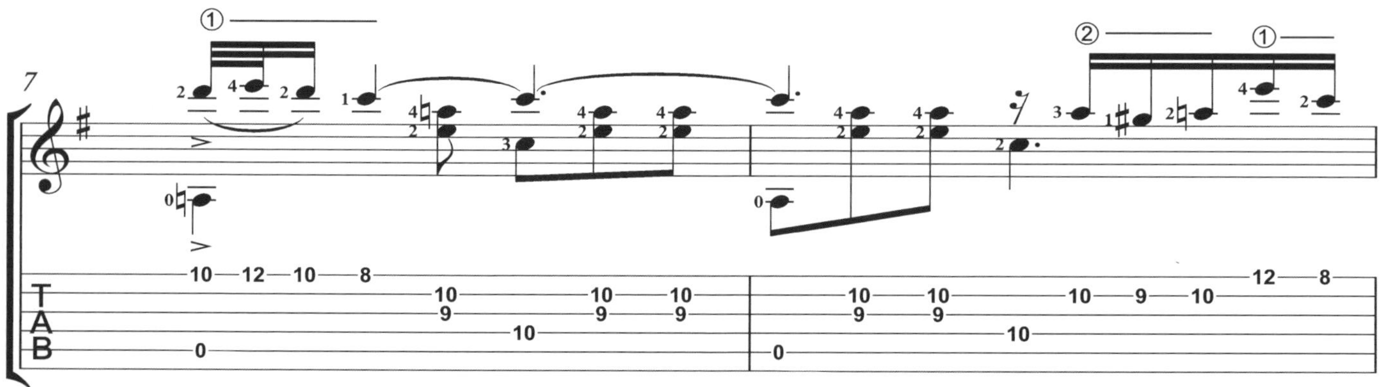

dim.
mp
f
dolce

dim.
mp
f

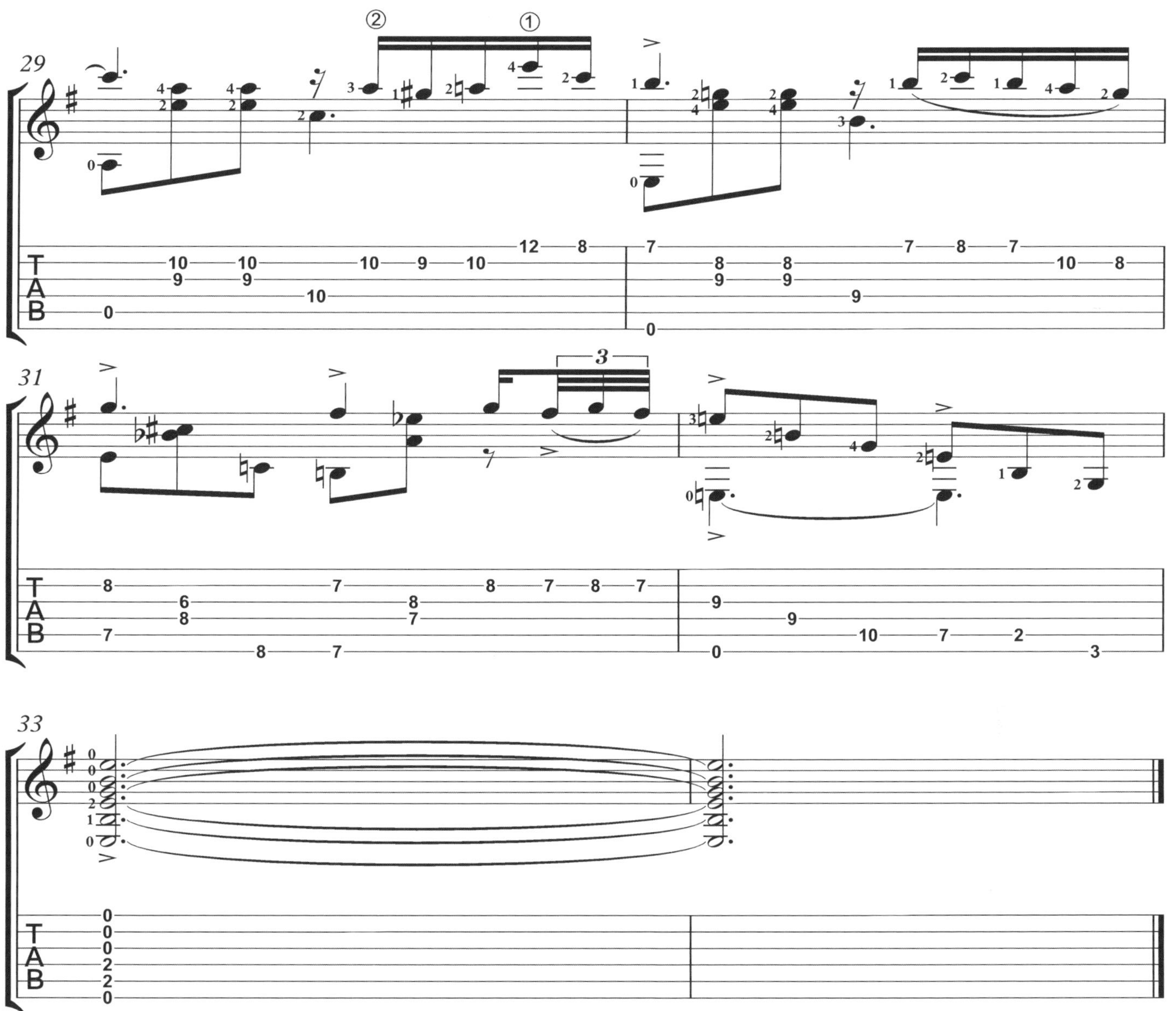
29
31
33

ETUDE XI

Ligado Study

Here, you will work with ligado technique
and left-hand extensions in F Ionian.

"I go where the guitar takes me."

Angus Young

Etude XI
Chords

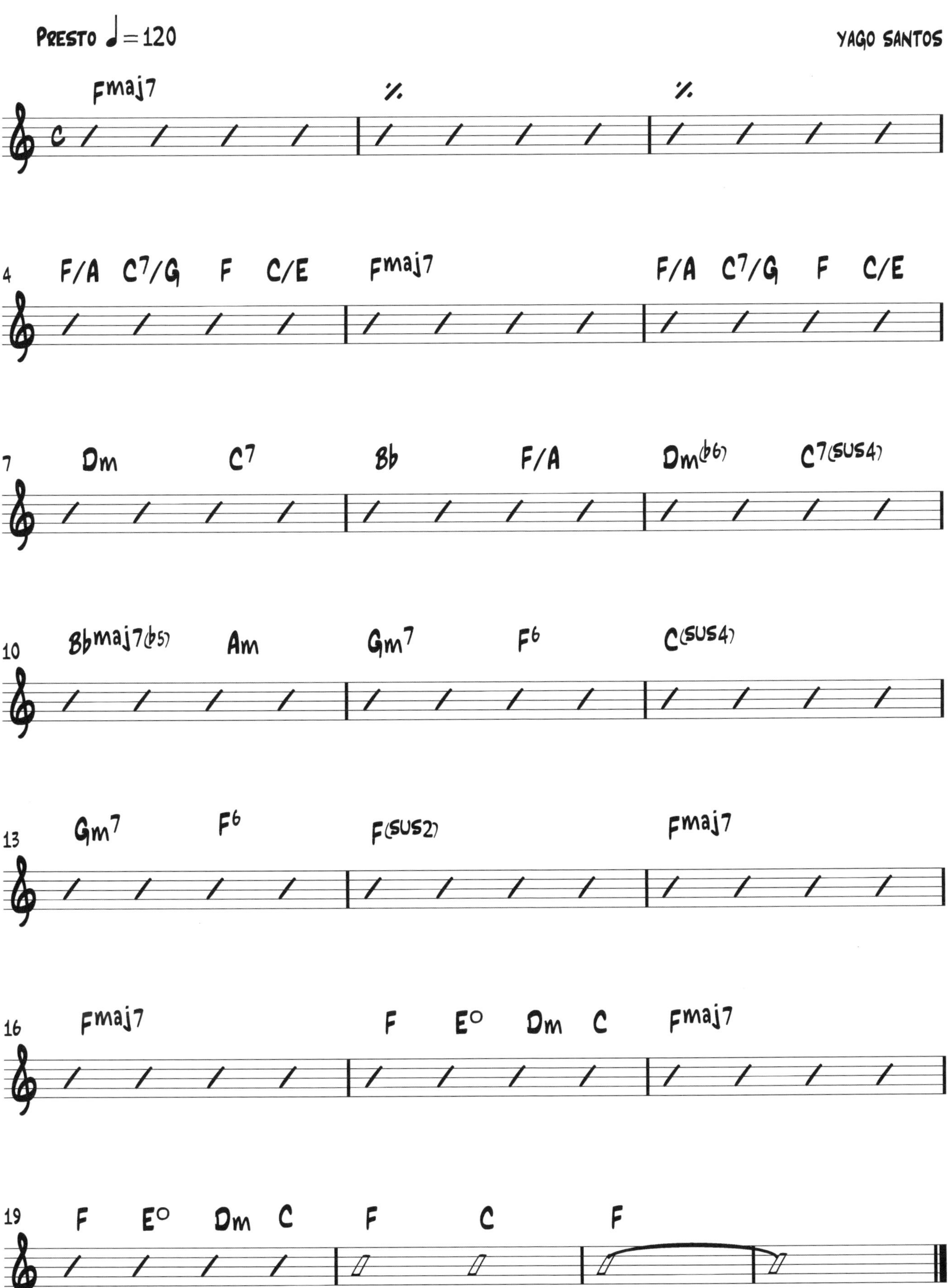

Etude XI

Presto ♩=120

Music and transcription by
YAGO SANTOS

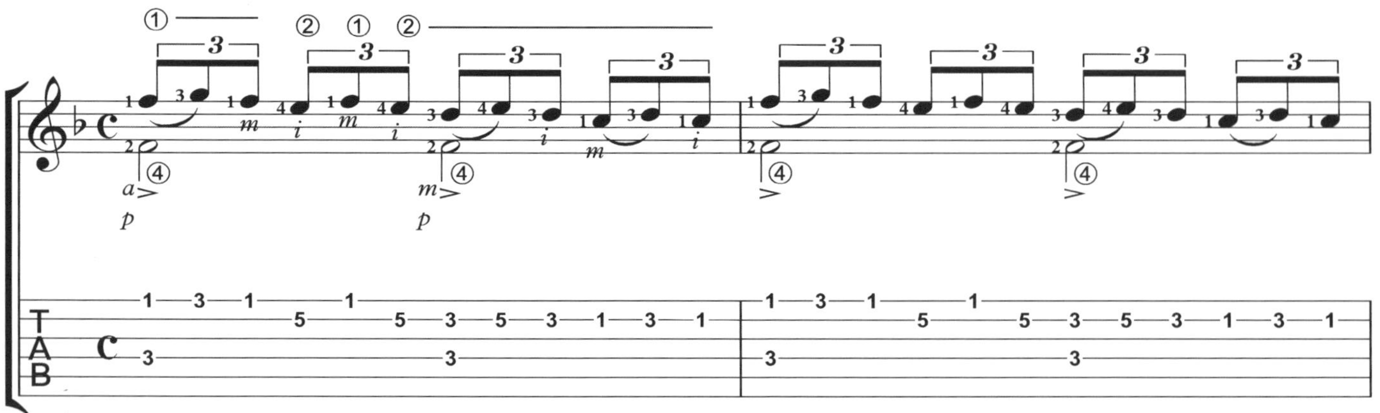

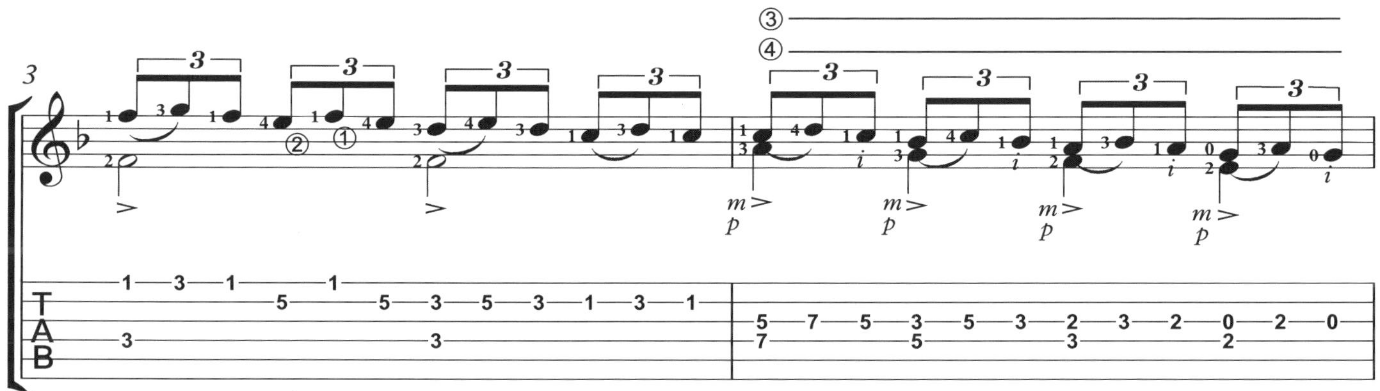

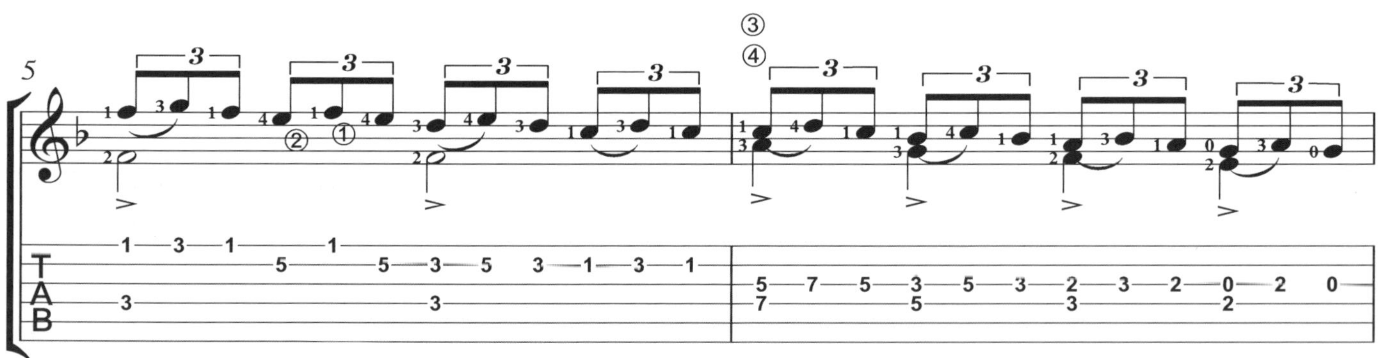

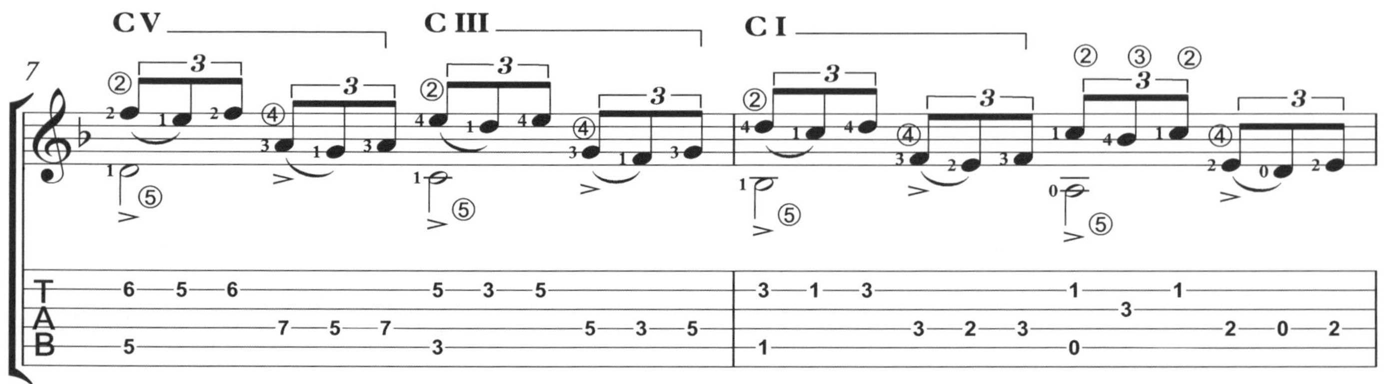

C V
C III
C I

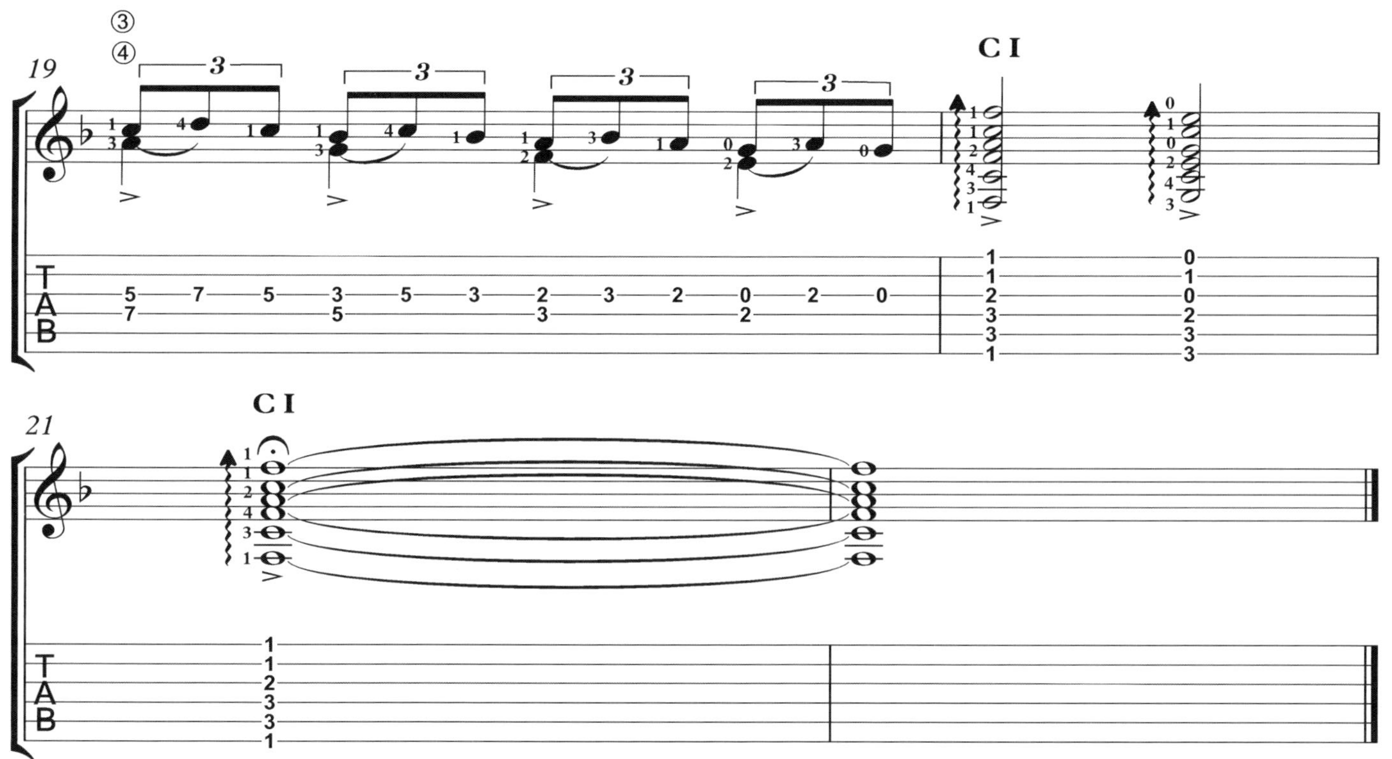
C I
C I

ETUDE XII

Arpeggio Study

Now you will work the right-hand pattern:
$p\,{}^{a}_{m}\,p\,{}^{m}_{i}\,p\,{}^{a}_{i}\,p\,{}^{m}_{i}$ in E Phrygian tonality (por arriba).

"You have a whole collection of musical ideas and thoughts that you have accumulated through your musical history, in addition to all the musical history of the world, and everything is in your subconscious. You feed on it when you play."

Joe Pass

Etude XII
Chords

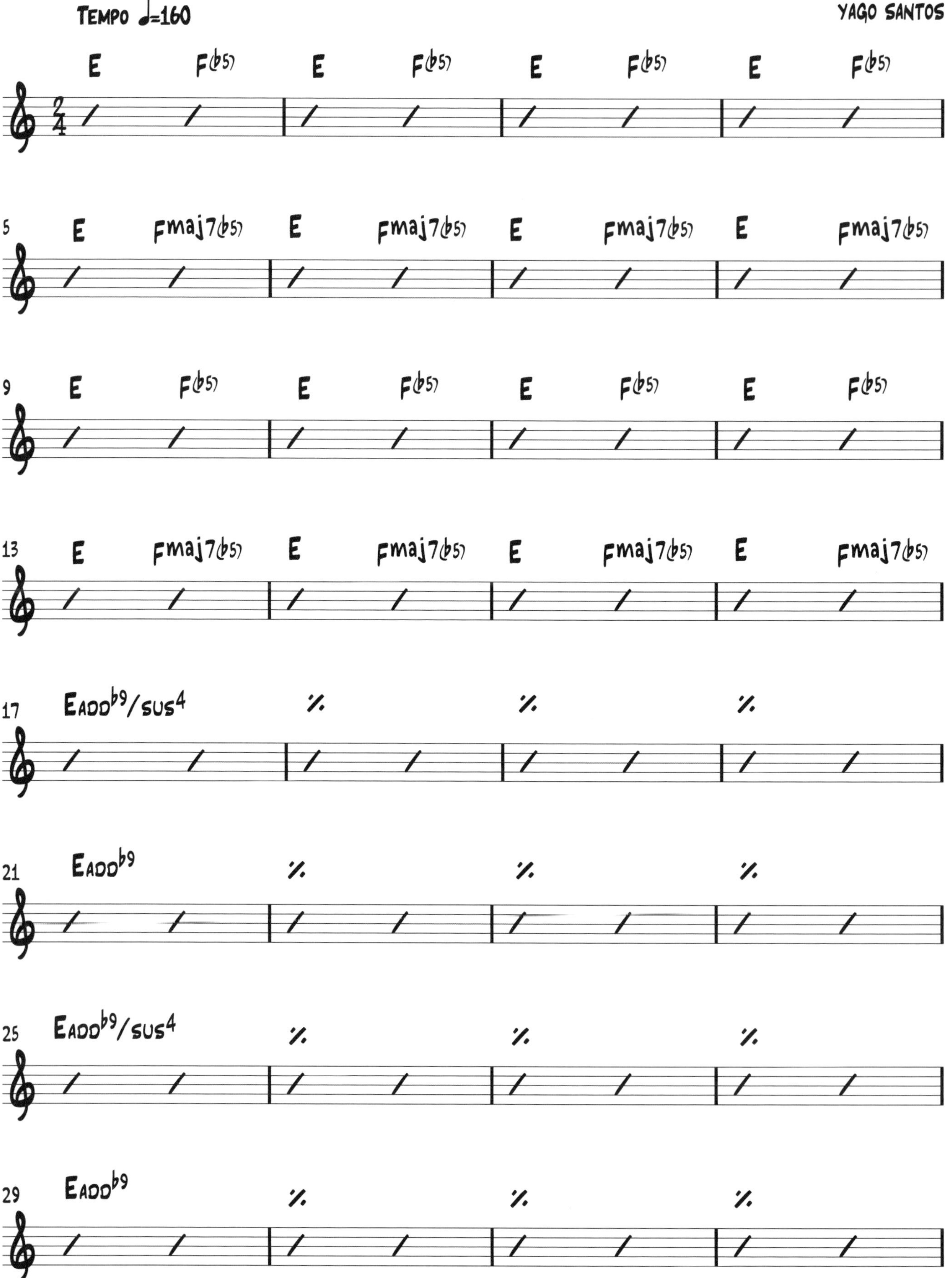

33
Dm(add9)
37
Cm(add9)
41
Am(add9)
45
Cm(add9)
Fmaj7(b5)
49
F7(b5)
Eadd b9
53
E
56

Etude XII

Tempo ♩=160

Music and transcription by
YAGO SANTOS

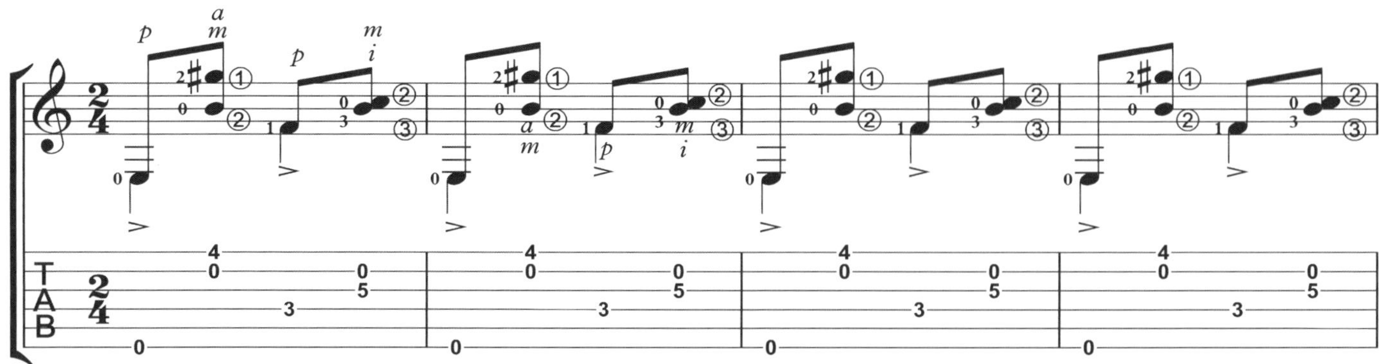

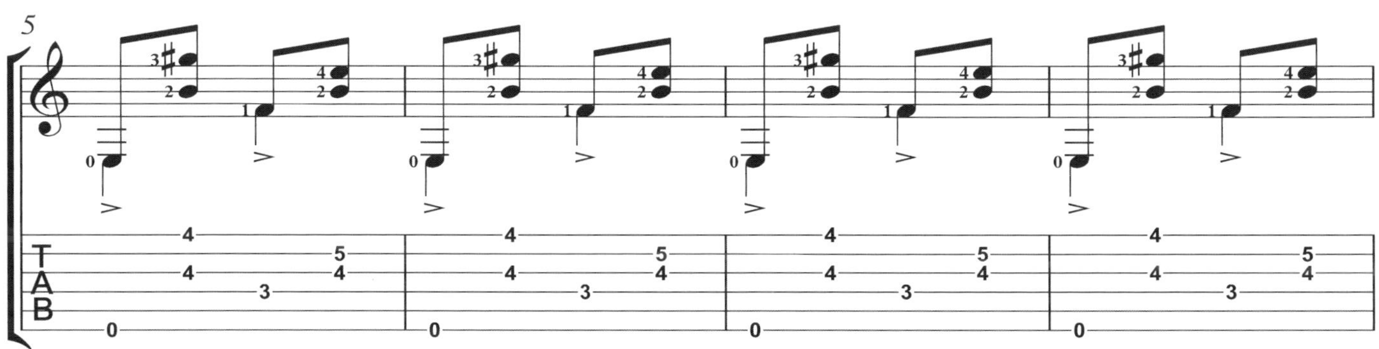

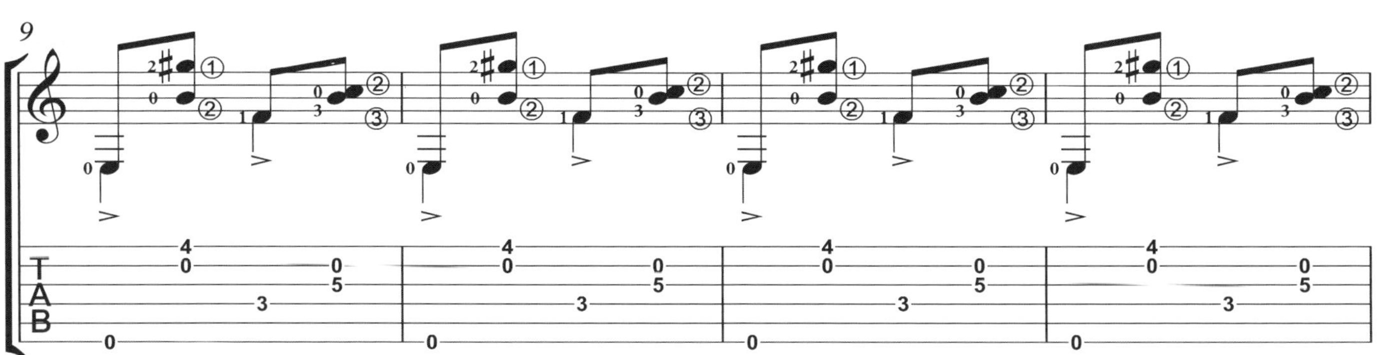

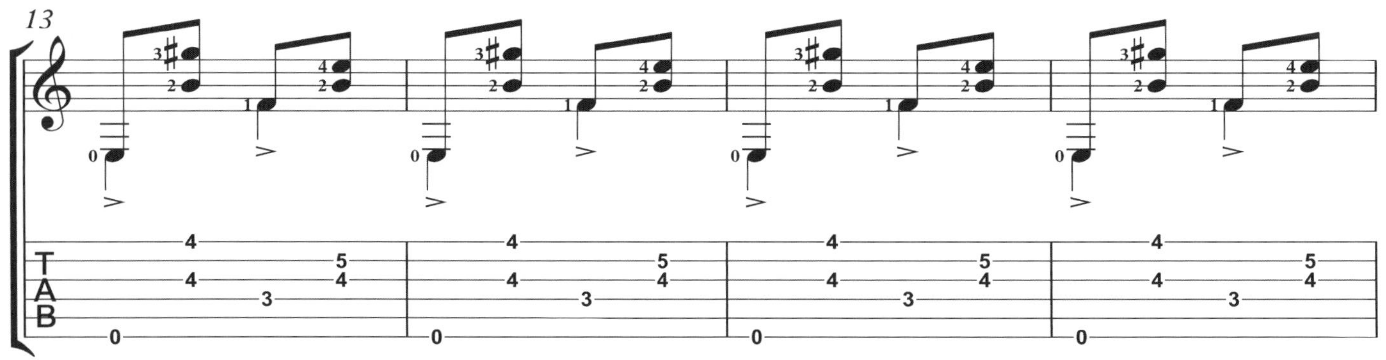

17
21
25
29
33
TAB

37
TAB
41
TAB
45
TAB
49
TAB
53
p p p i
m a m i
TAB

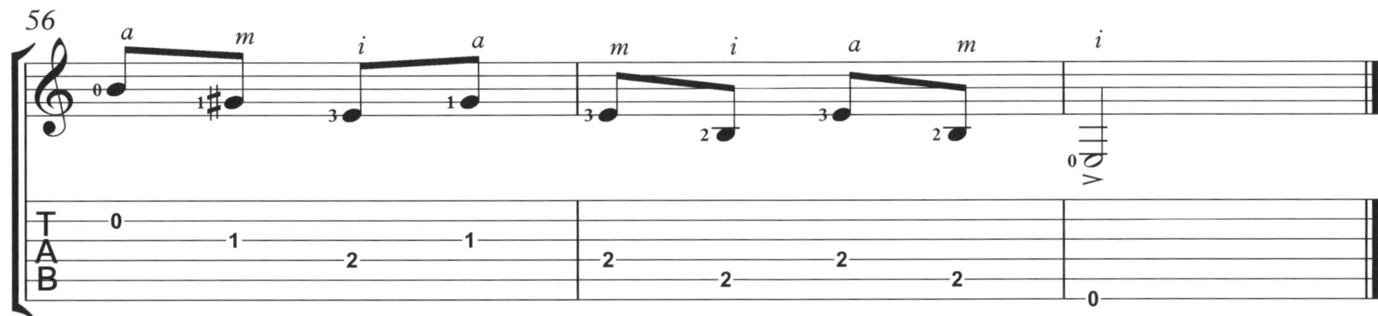
56
a
m
i
a
m
i
a
m
i
T
A
B

ETUDE XIII

Warm-Up Study

Now we'll practice arpeggio, picado and the *i m a m* and $i\ {}^{a}_{m}\ {}^{a}_{m}\ {}^{a}_{m}$ patterns in A Ionian/Aeolian.

"Listening is the key to everything good in music."

Pat Metheny

Etude XIII
Chords

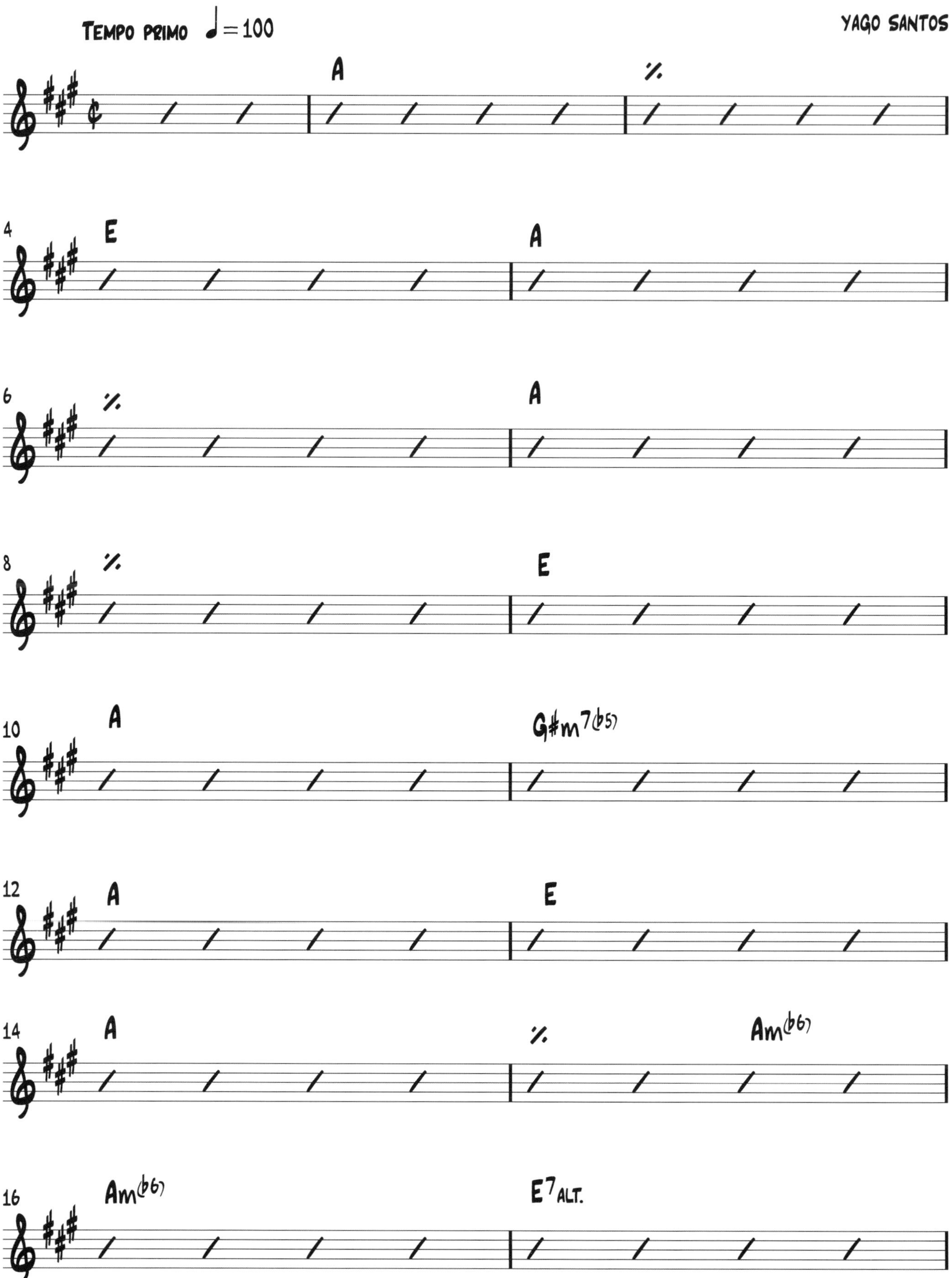

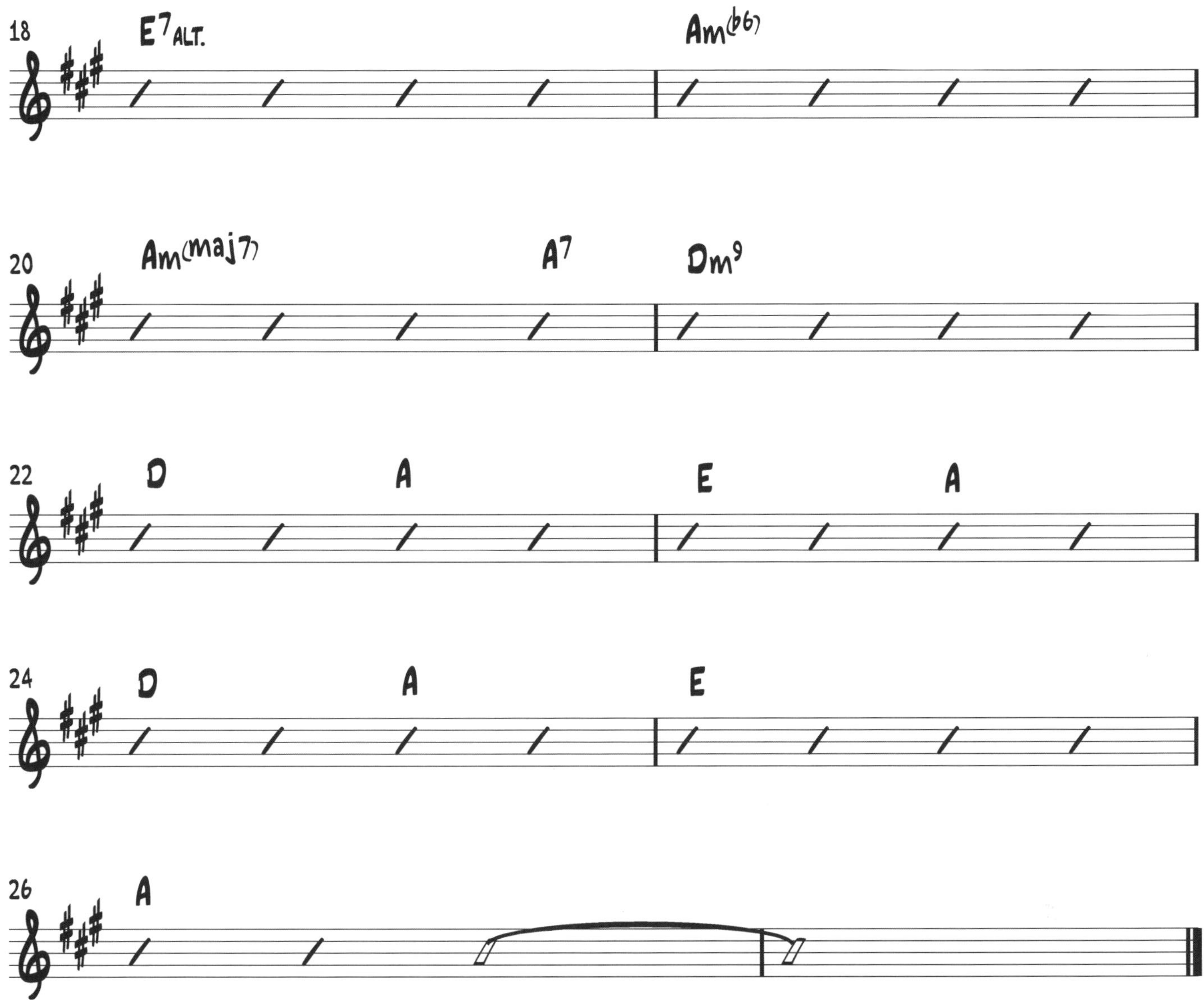
18
E7ALT.
Am(b6)
20
Am(maj7)
A7
Dm9
22
D
A
E
A
24
D
A
E
26
A

Etude XIII

Music and transcription by
YAGO SANTOS

Tempo primo ♩=100

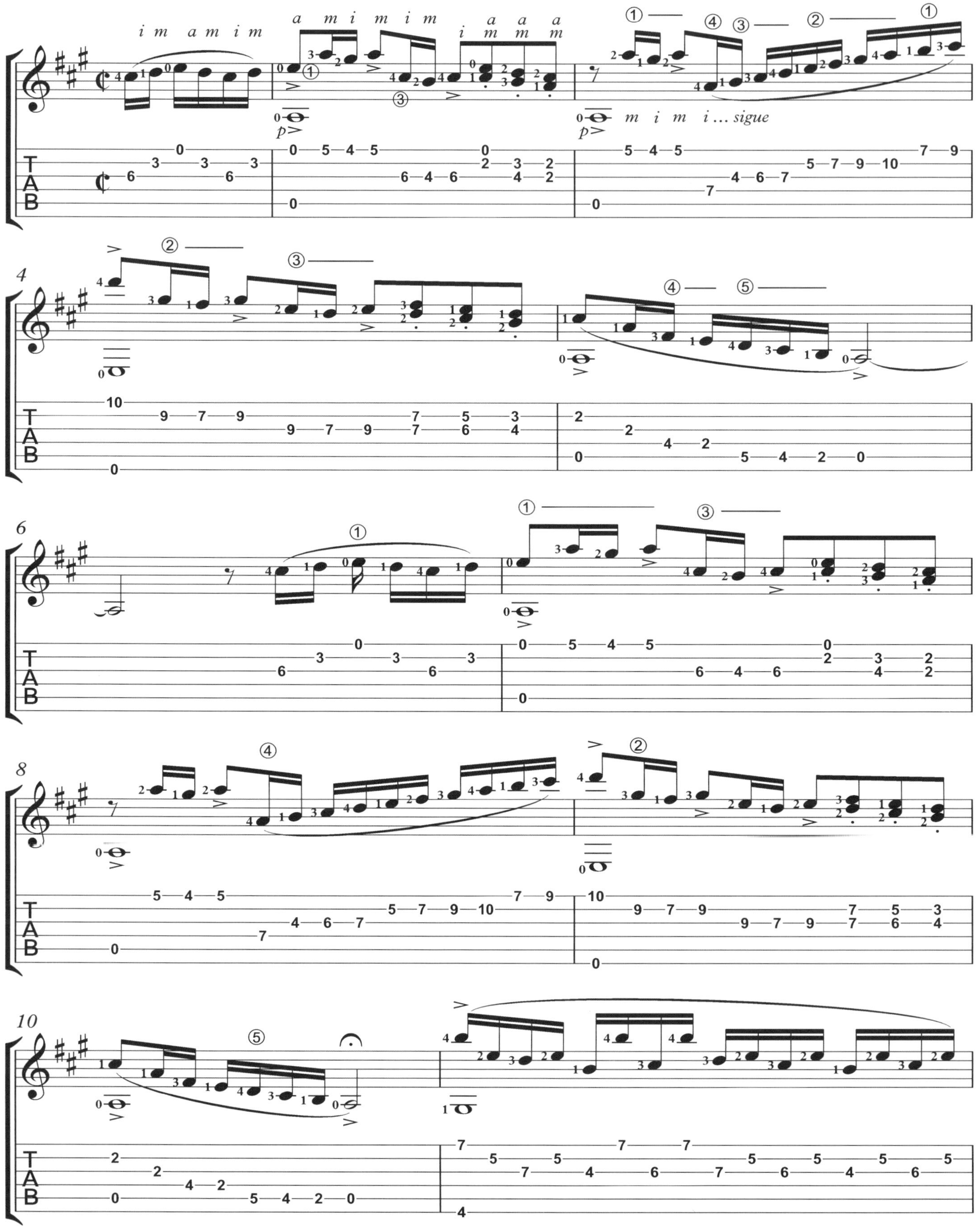

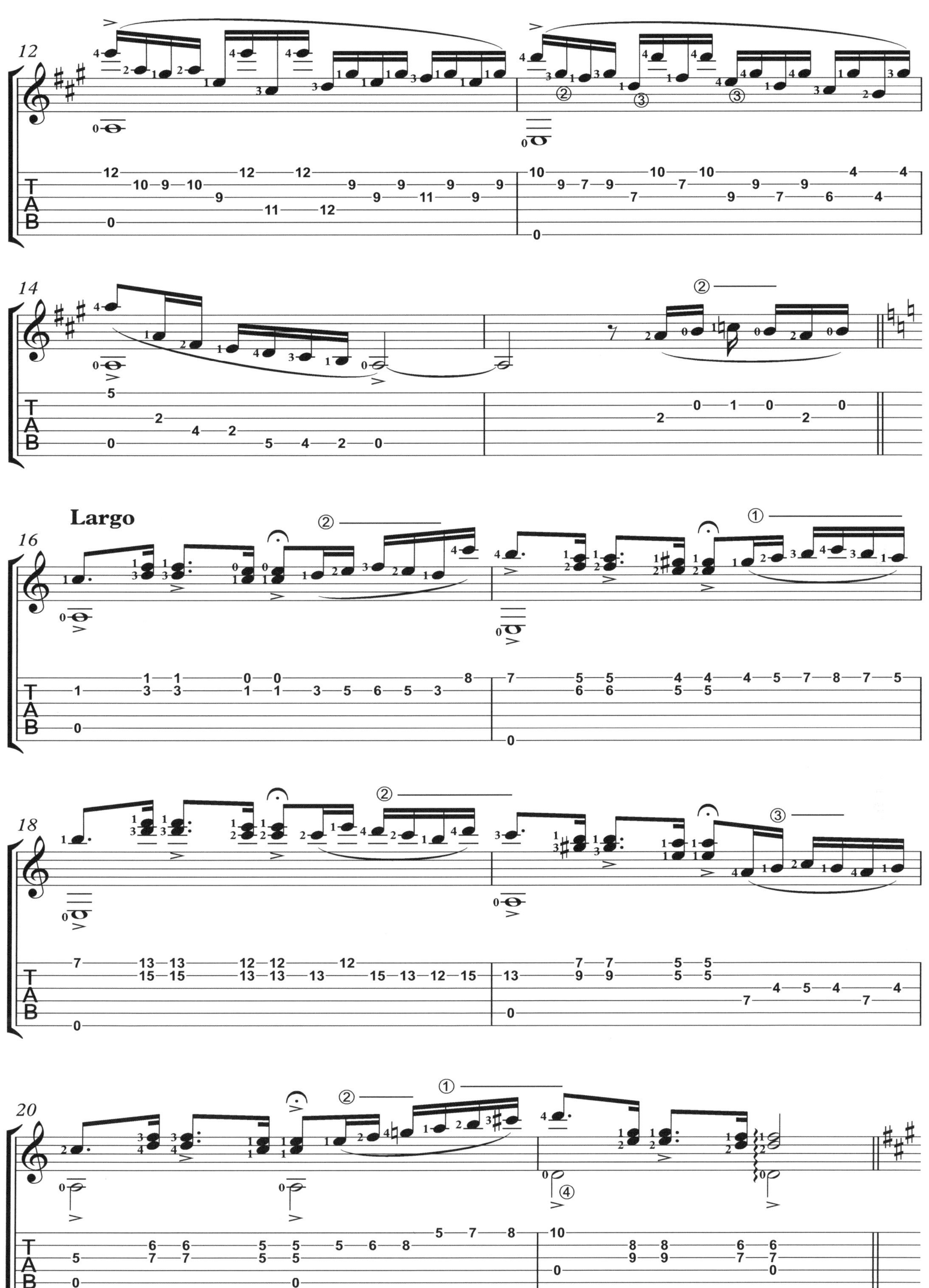
Largo

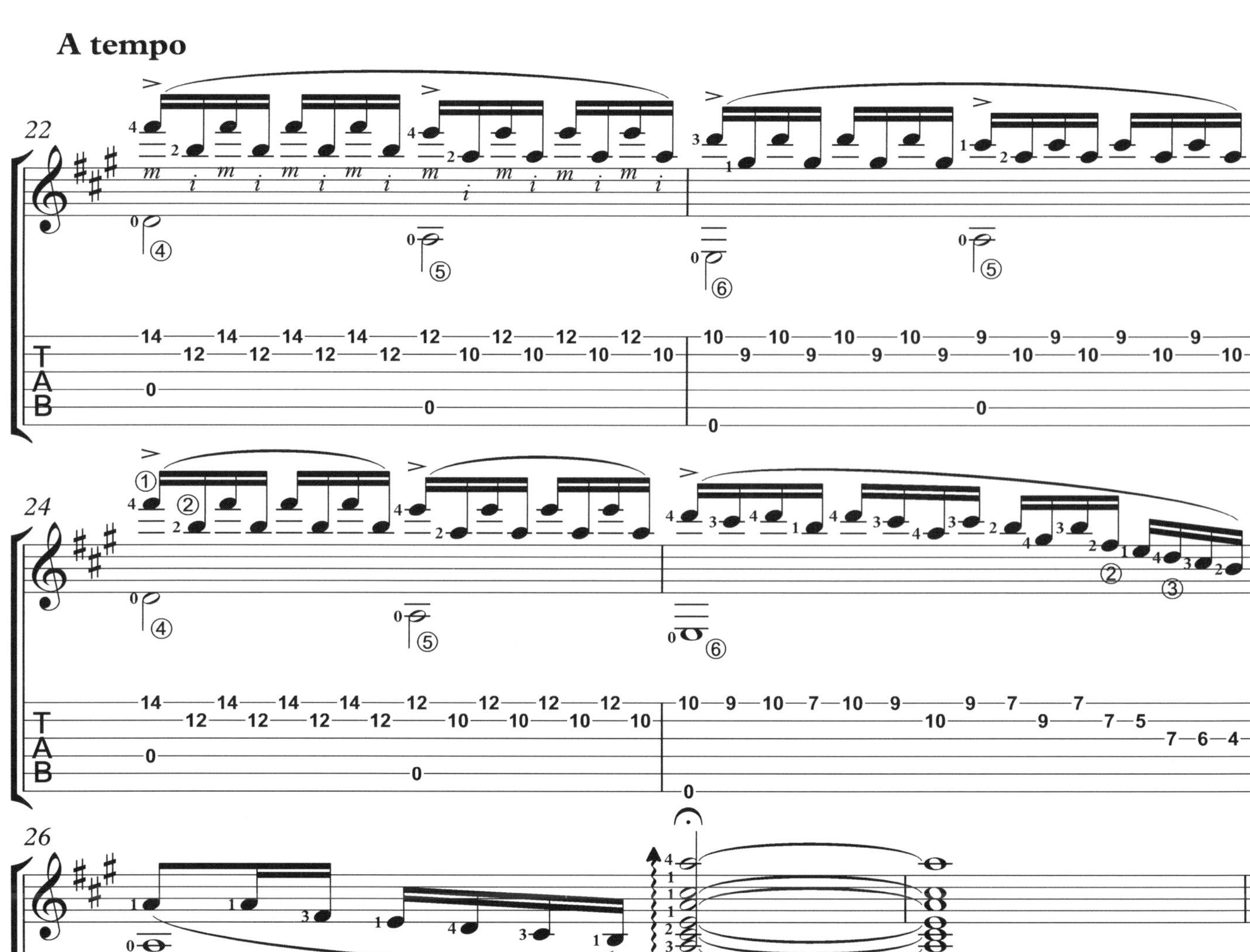
A tempo

ETUDE XIV

6th in D

In this etude, you will practice the arpeggio, picado and ligado techniques in D Aeolian. The scordatura tuning adds depth to the harmony.

"If you play music for no other reason
than simply because you love it,
little by little the skills will come to you
without realizing it."

Nuno Bettencourt

Etude XIV
Chords

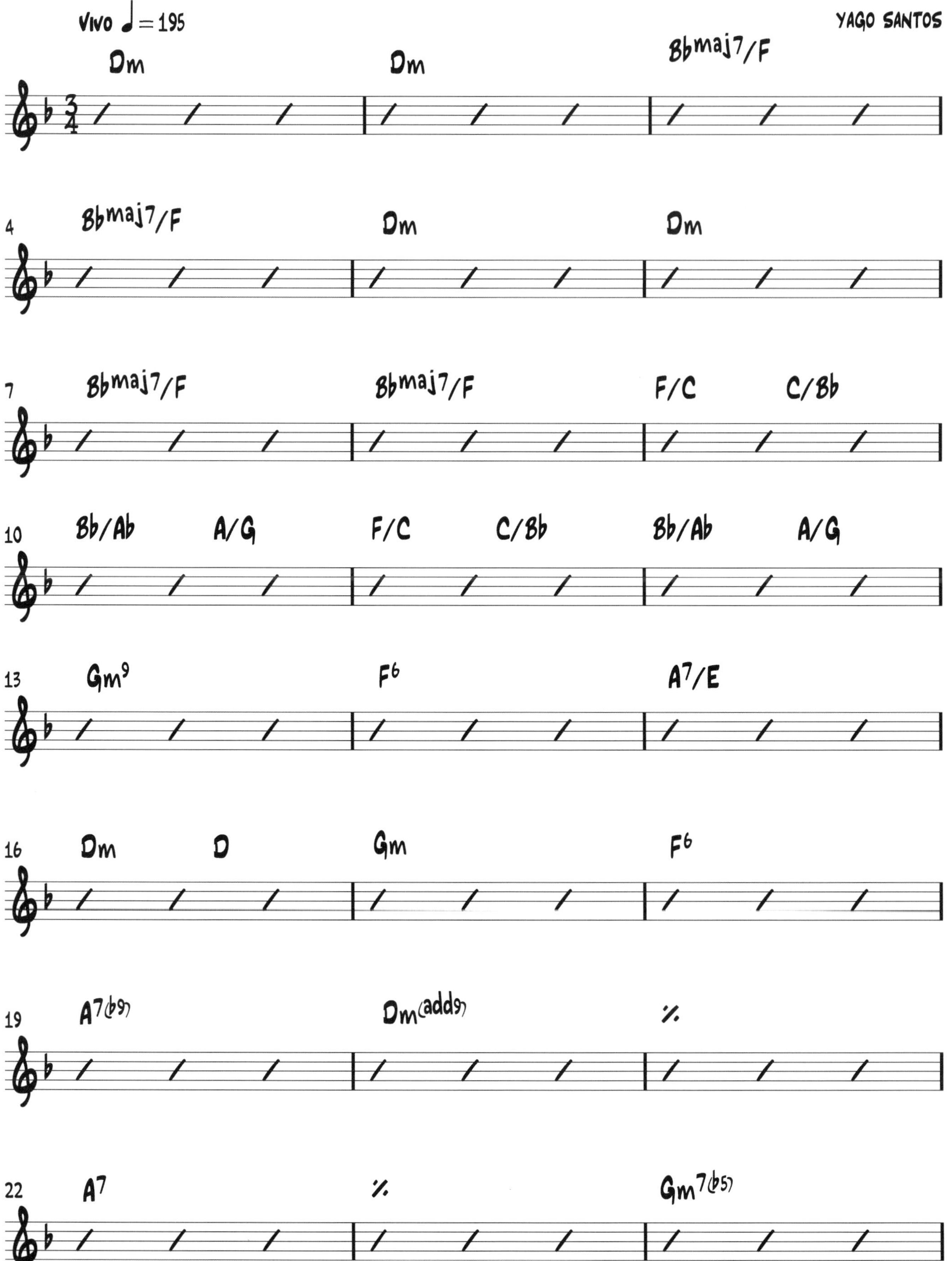

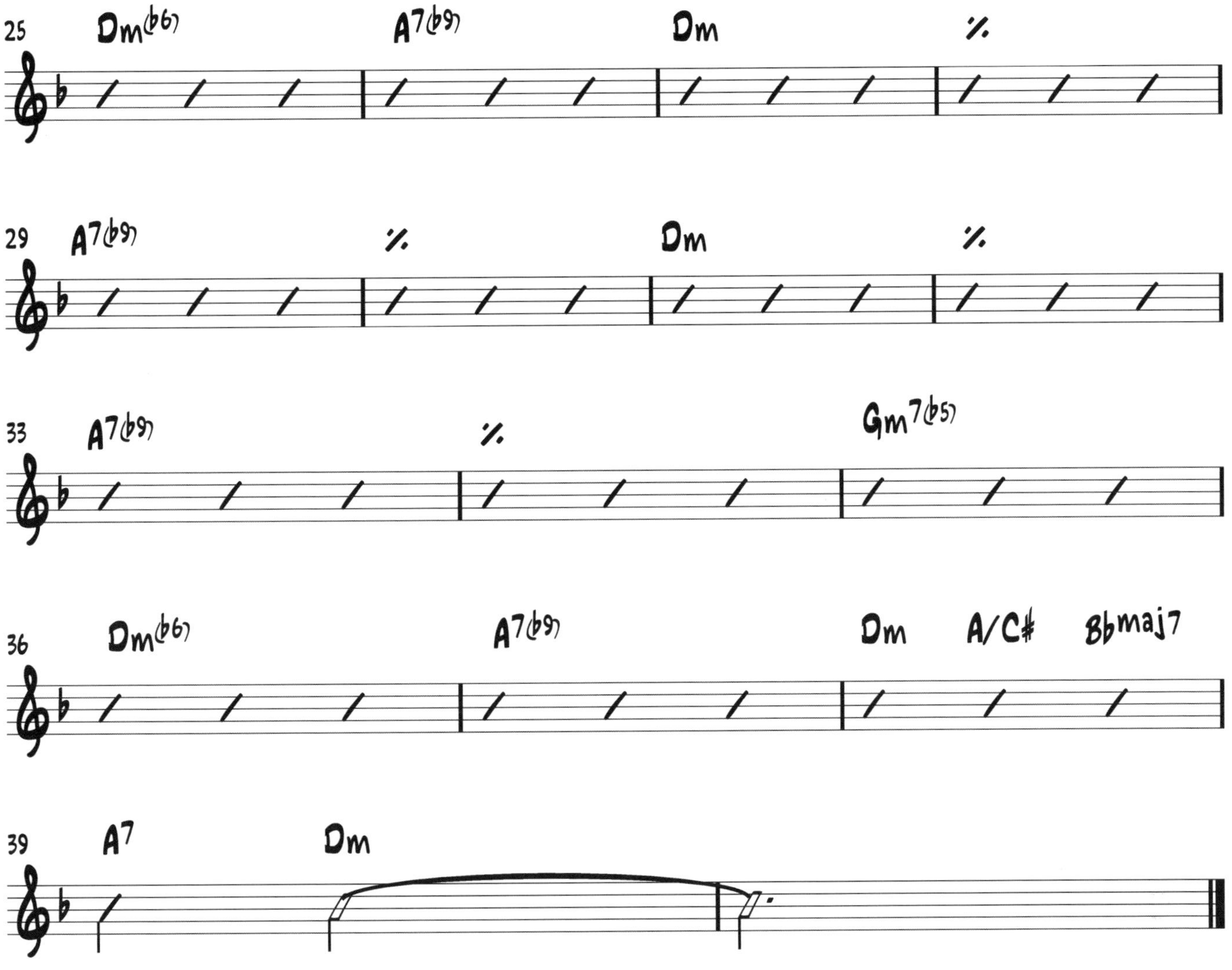

25
Dm(b6)
A7(b9)
Dm
%
29
A7(b9)
%
Dm
%
33
A7(b9)
%
Gm7(b5)
36
Dm(b6)
A7(b9)
Dm
A/C#
Bbmaj7
39
A7
Dm

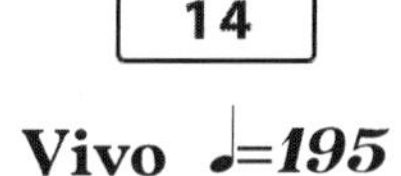

Etude XIV

Music and transcription by
YAGO SANTOS

Vivo ♩=195

⑥ —— D

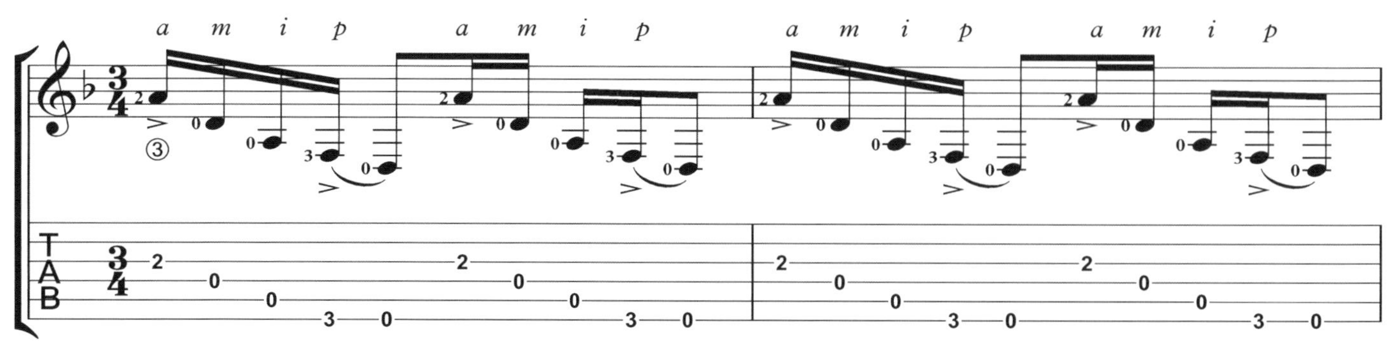

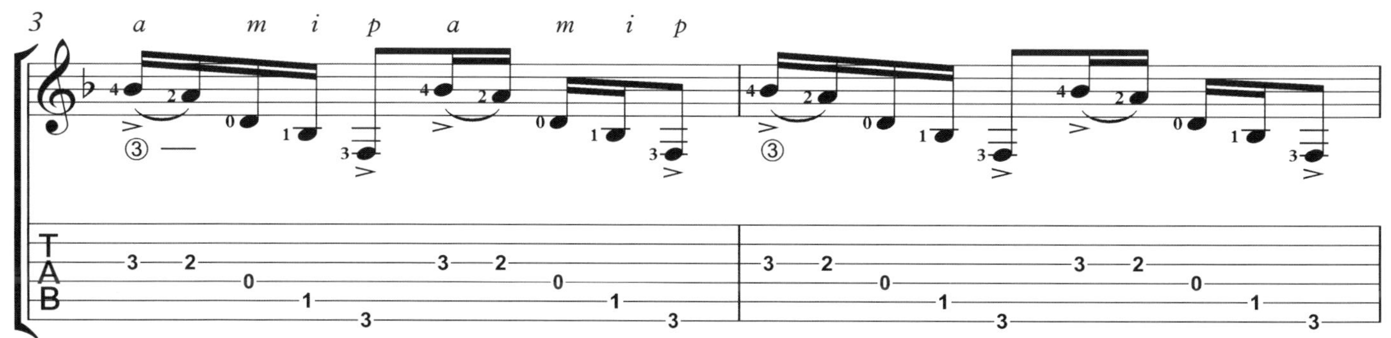

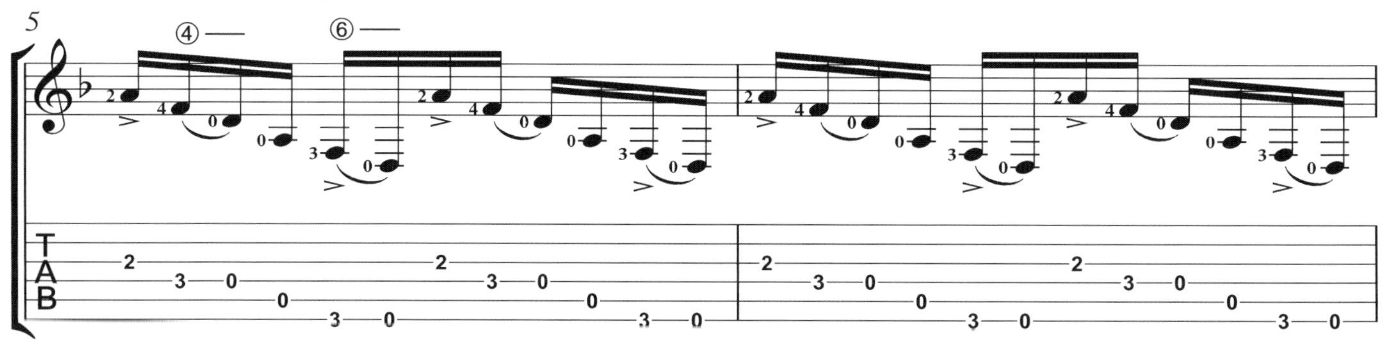

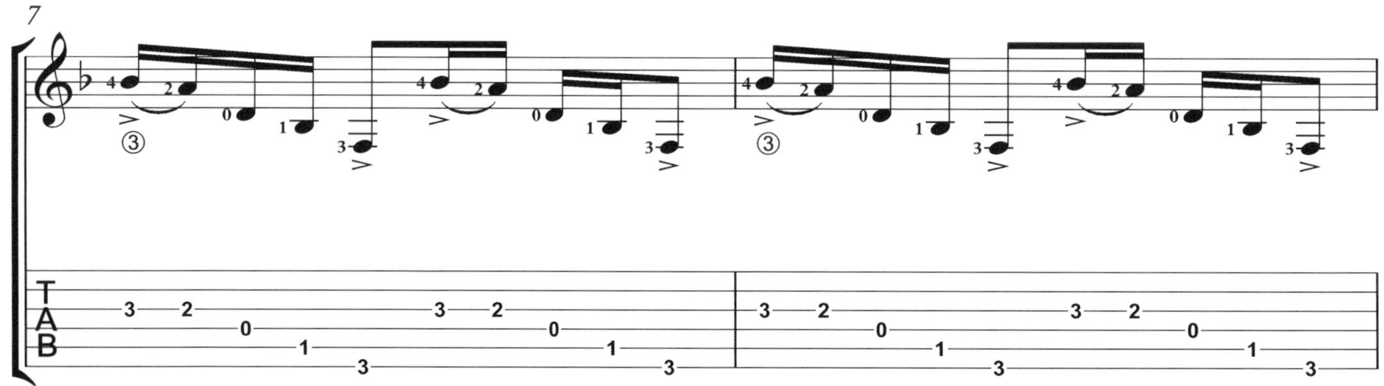

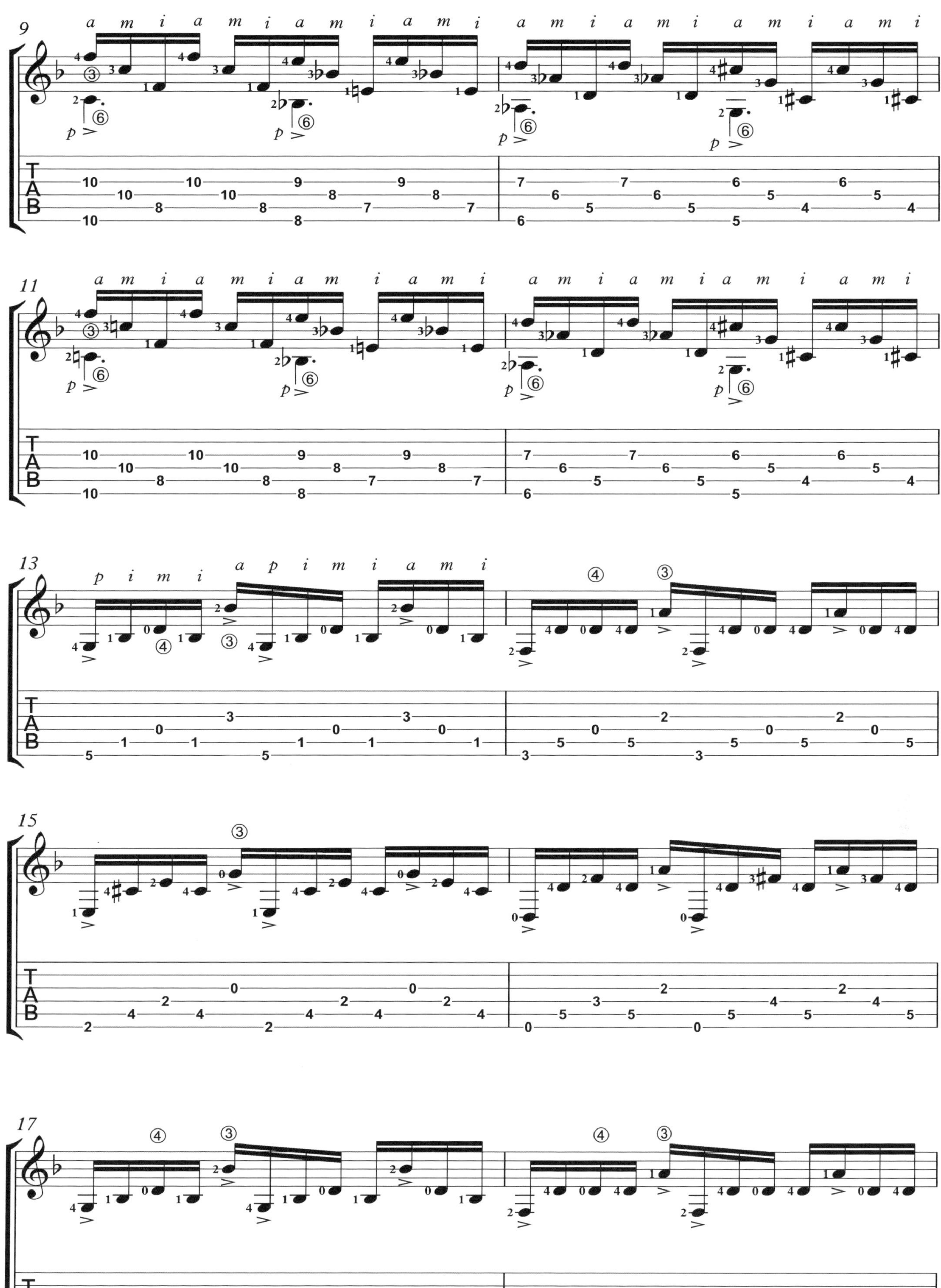
9
a m i a m i a m i a m i a m i a m i a m i a m i
11
a m i a m i a m i a m i a m i a m i a m i a m i
13
p i m i a p i m i a m i
15
17
T
A
B

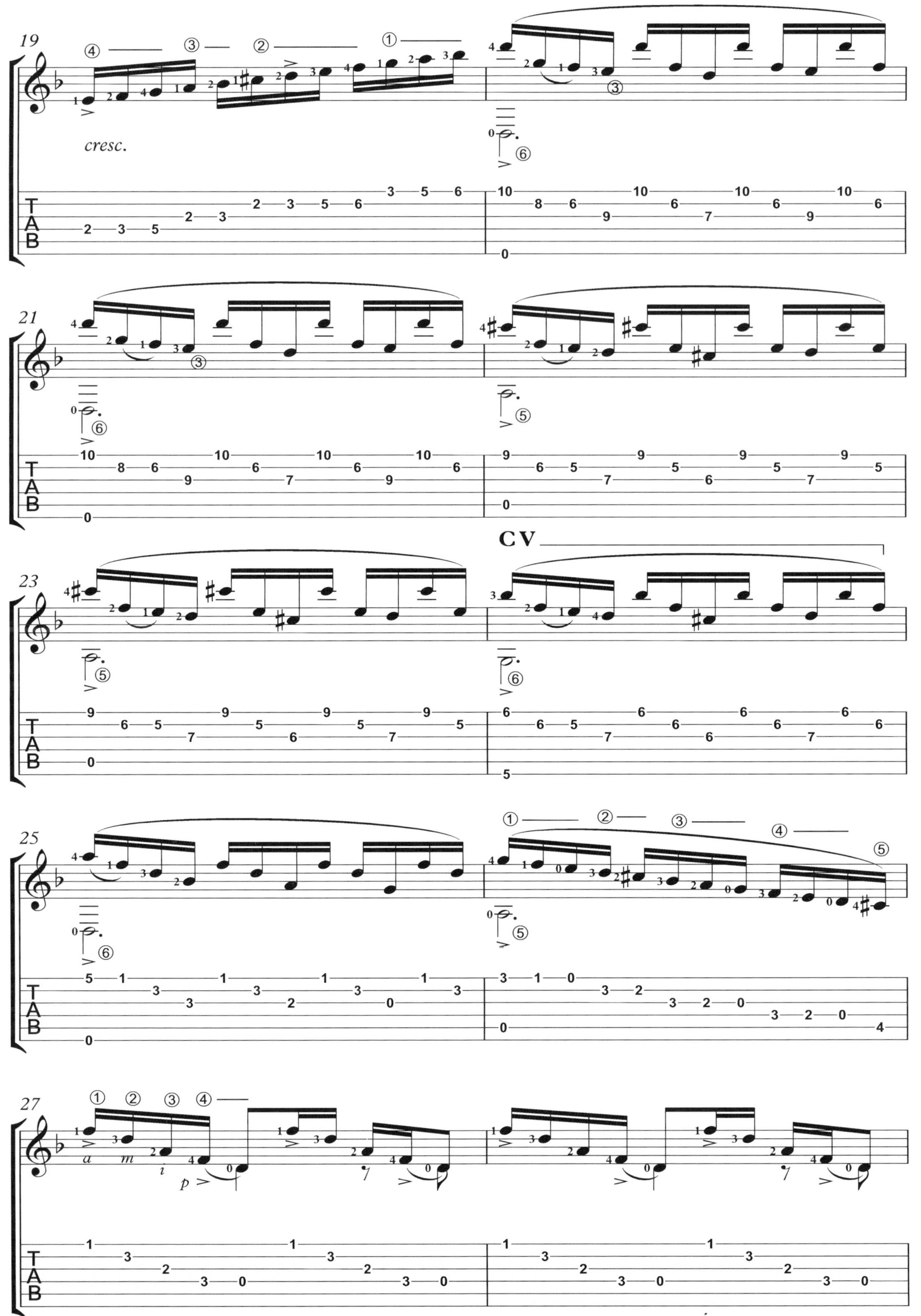
cresc.
CV

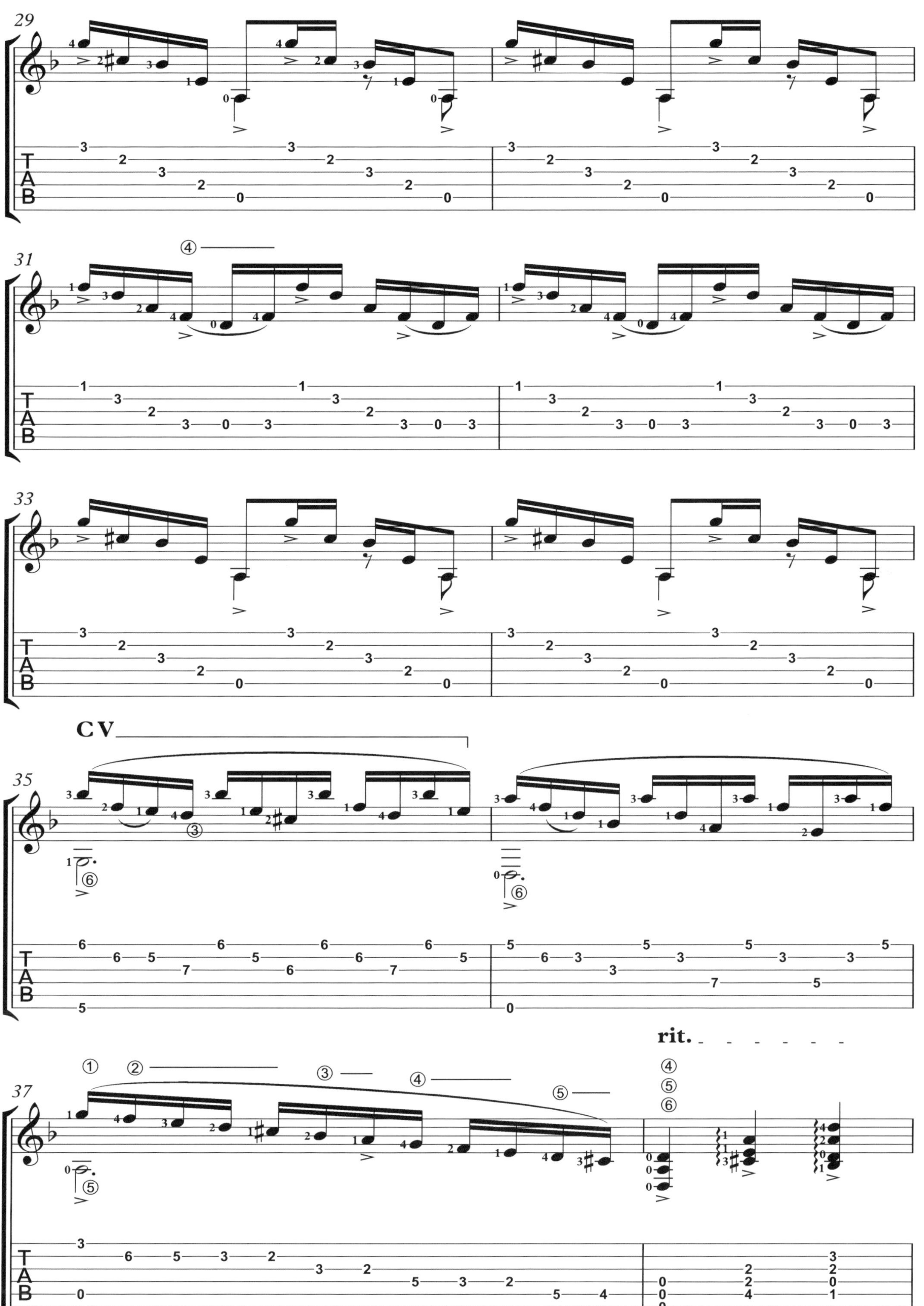
29
31
33
CV
35
rit.
37
T
A
B

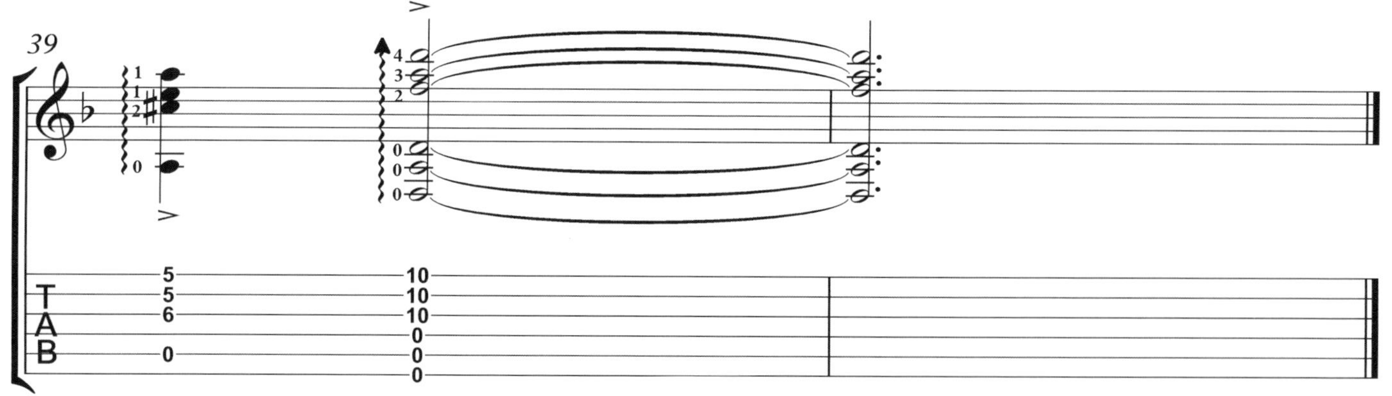
39
TAB

ETUDE XV

Double-Arpeggio Study

This study uses double-arpeggio
technique in D♯ Phrygian.

*"My guitar is not a thing.
It is an extension of myself.
It is what I am."*

Joan Jett

Etude XV
Chords

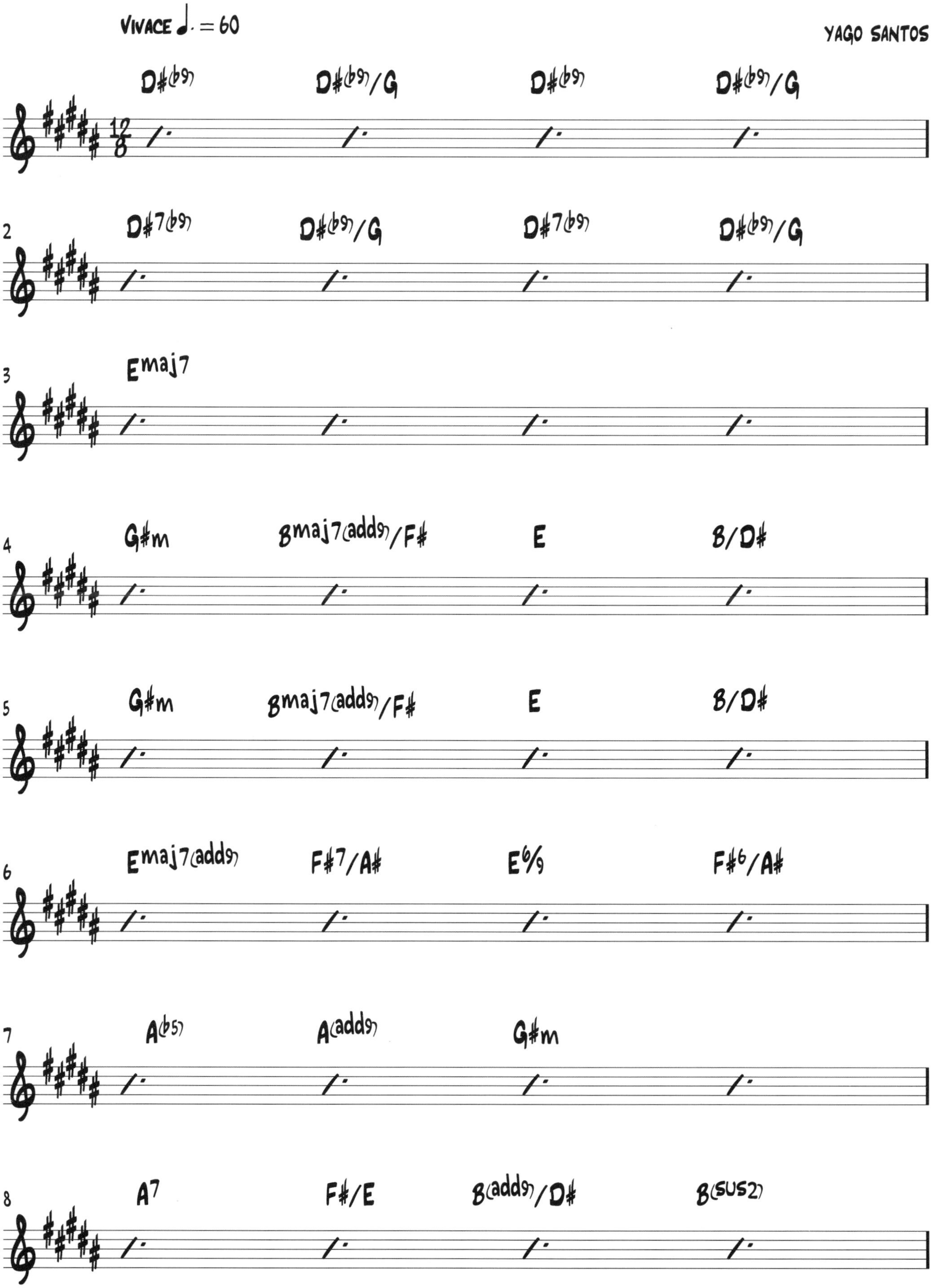

VIVACE ♩. = 60

YAGO SANTOS

D#(b9) | D#(b9)/G | D#(b9) | D#(b9)/G

2 D#7(b9) | D#(b9)/G | D#7(b9) | D#(b9)/G

3 Emaj7

4 G#m | Bmaj7(add9)/F# | E | B/D#

5 G#m | Bmaj7(add9)/F# | E | B/D#

6 Emaj7(add9) | F#7/A# | E6/9 | F#6/A#

7 A(b5) | A(add9) | G#m

8 A7 | F#/E | B(add9)/D# | B(sus2)

9
C#m(add9)
Emaj7/G#
G#m(add9)
Bmaj7
10
Bmaj7/F#
Bmaj7/C#
Emaj7(add13)
11
C#m
C#m/G#
F#7(add4)
Bmaj7(add4)
12
Emaj7(add9)
F#6/A#
E6/9
F#7/A#
13
A(b5)
A(add9)
G#m
14
A7
F#/E
B(add9)/D#
B(sus2)
15
C#m(add9)
Emaj7/G#
G#m(add9)
Bmaj7
16
Bmaj7/F#
Bmaj7/C#
Emaj7(add13)
17
D#(b9)/G

Etude XV

Music and transcription by
YAGO SANTOS

Vivace ♩.=*60*

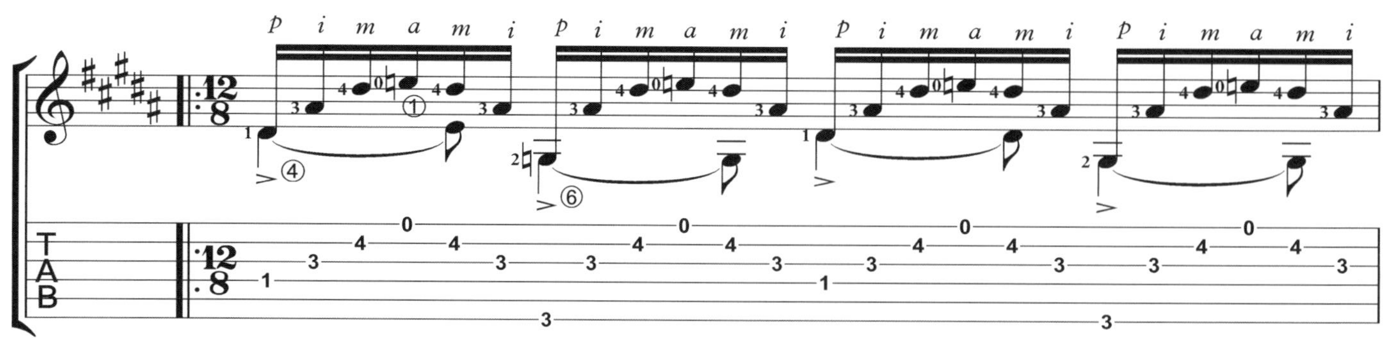

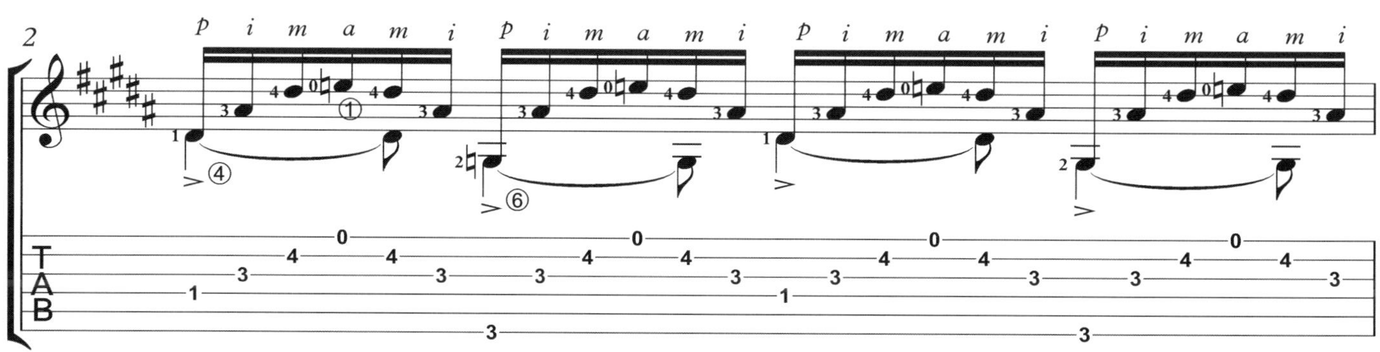

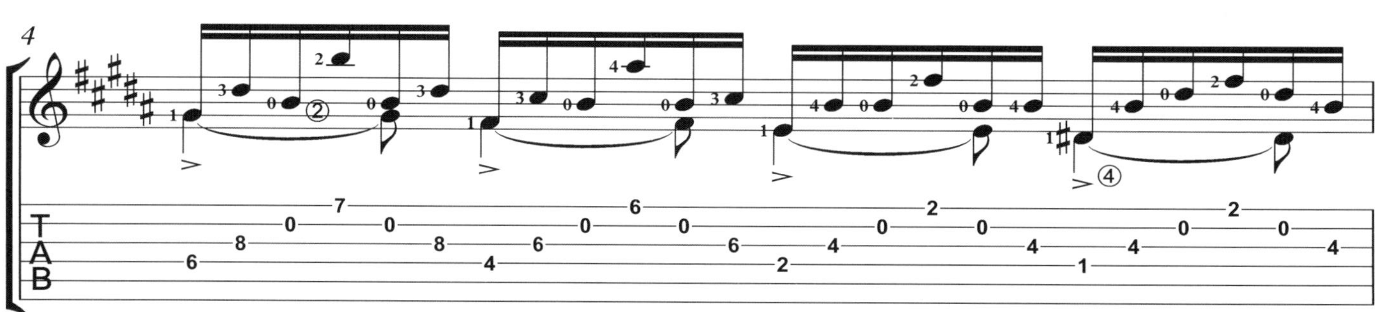

C VII
C IV
p m i a i m p i m a m i
TAB

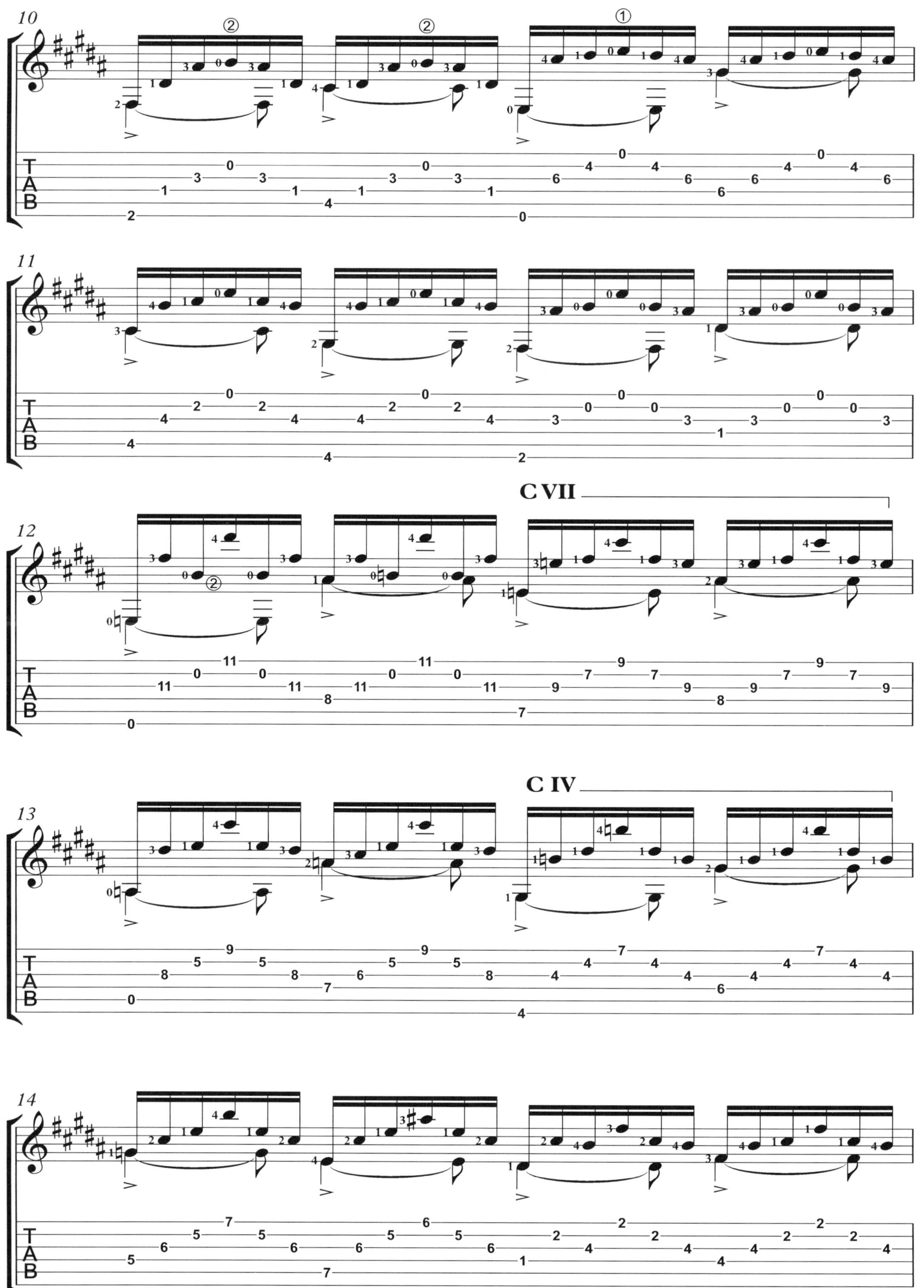
10
11
12
C VII
13
C IV
14

15
p m i a i m p i m a m i
16
17
TAB

ETUDE XVI

Tremolo Study

This study uses the quintuplet flamenco tremolo technique in A Aeolian.

"I dedicated all the time I had to [the guitar]. The 10-hour workout was just what I put in the magazine [Guitar World] at the time [1990], but for me - it was every waking moment."

Steve Vai

Etude XVI

Presto ♩=130

Music and transcription by
YAGO SANTOS

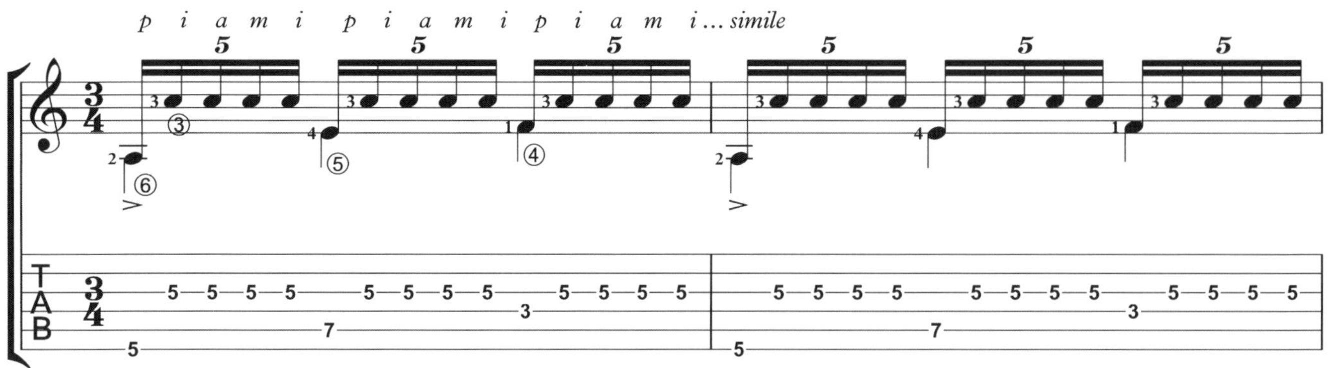

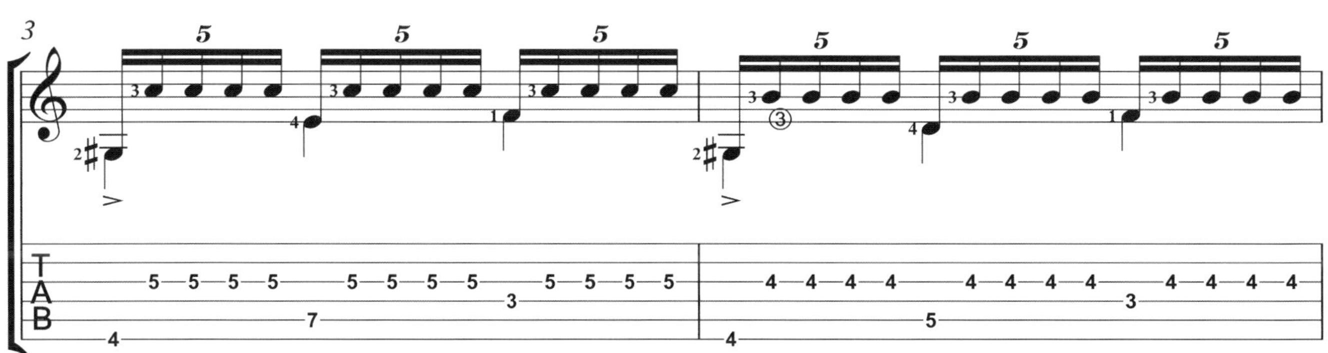

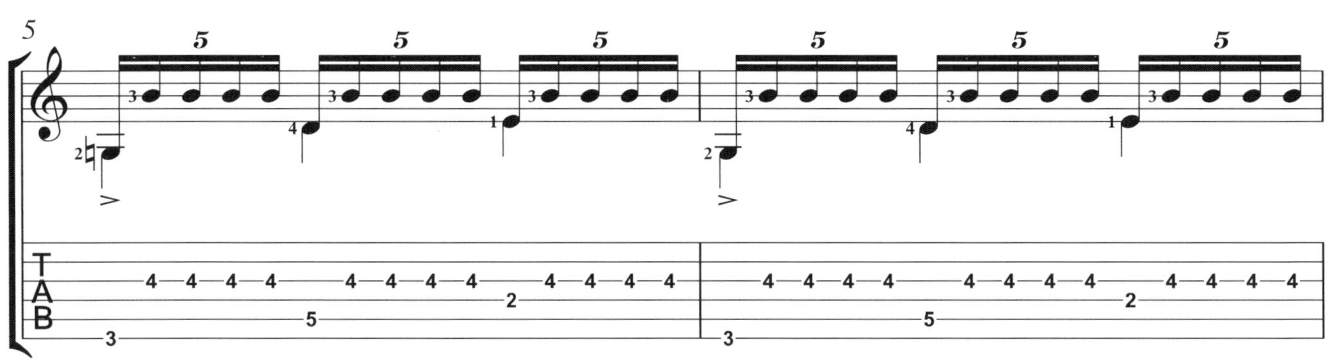

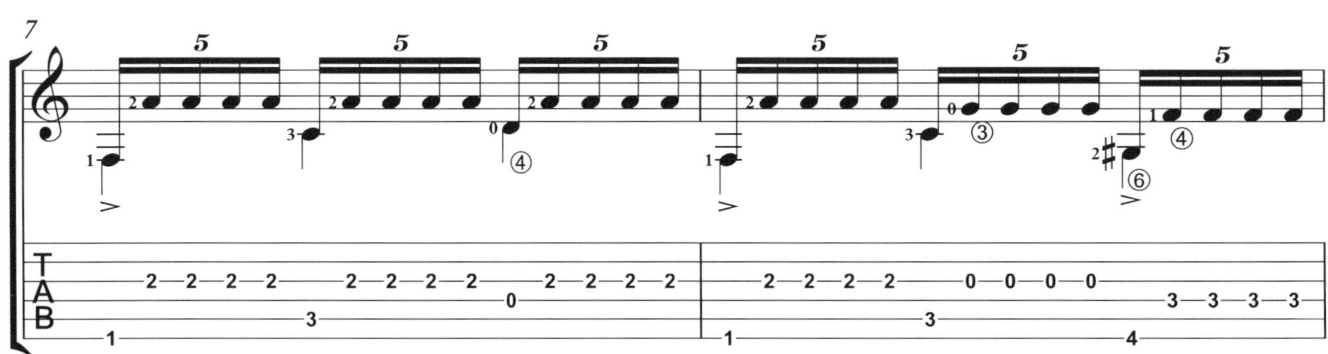

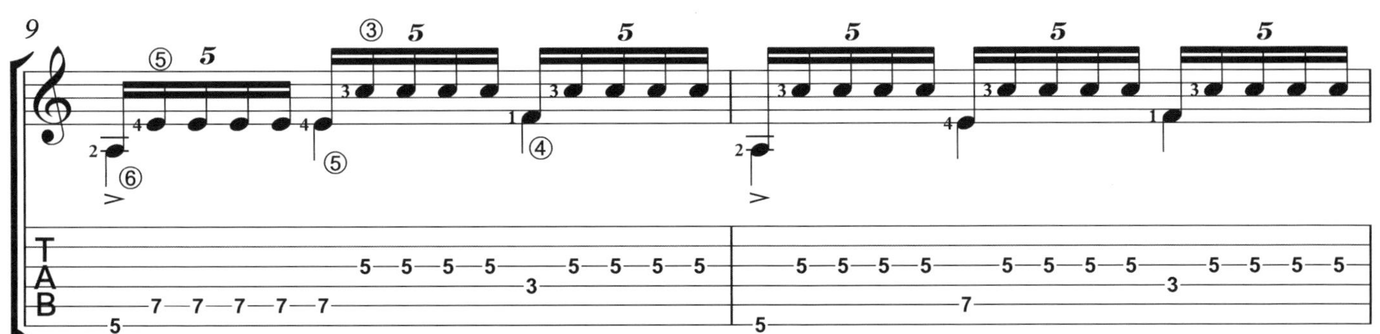
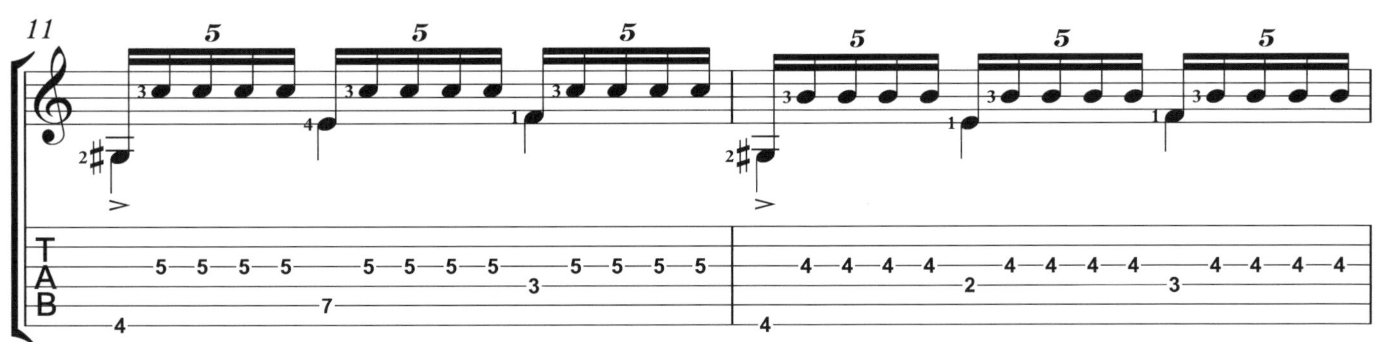
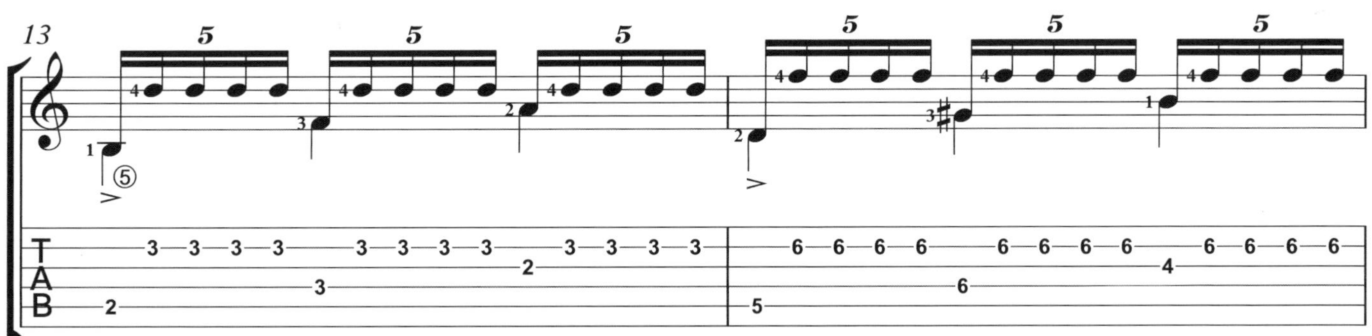
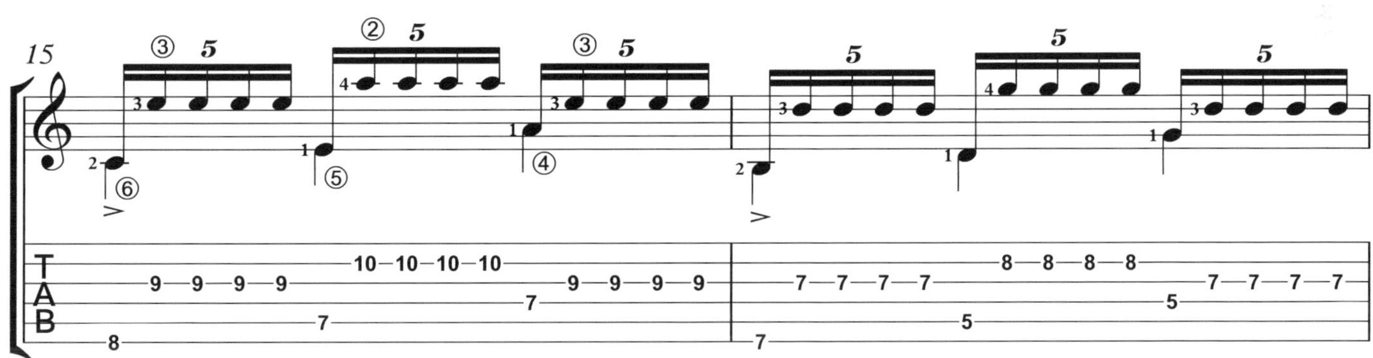
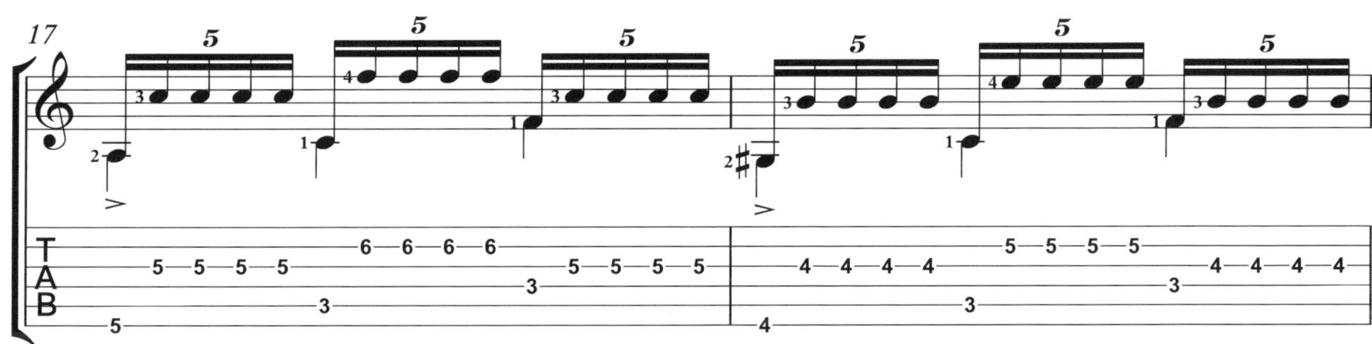

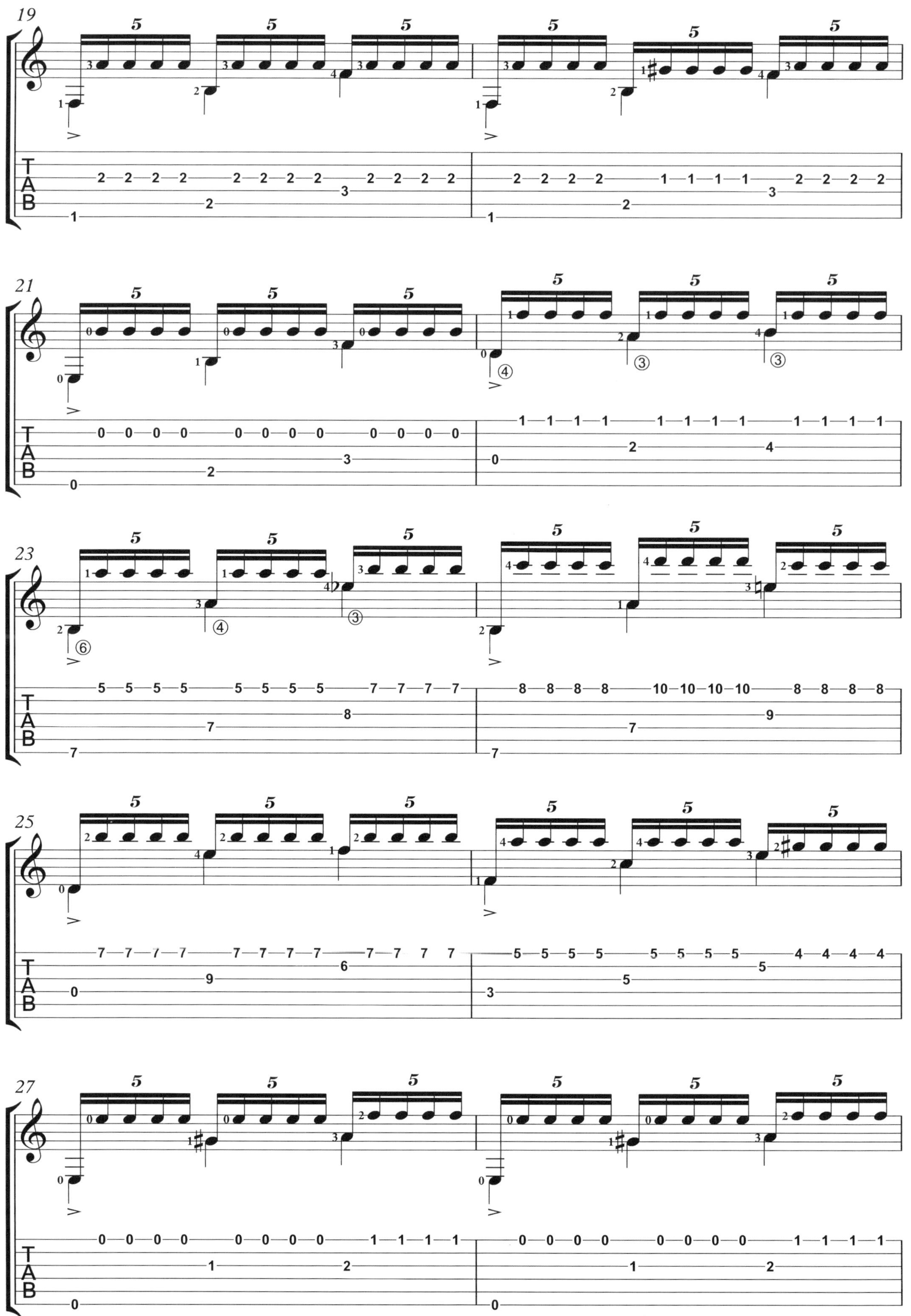

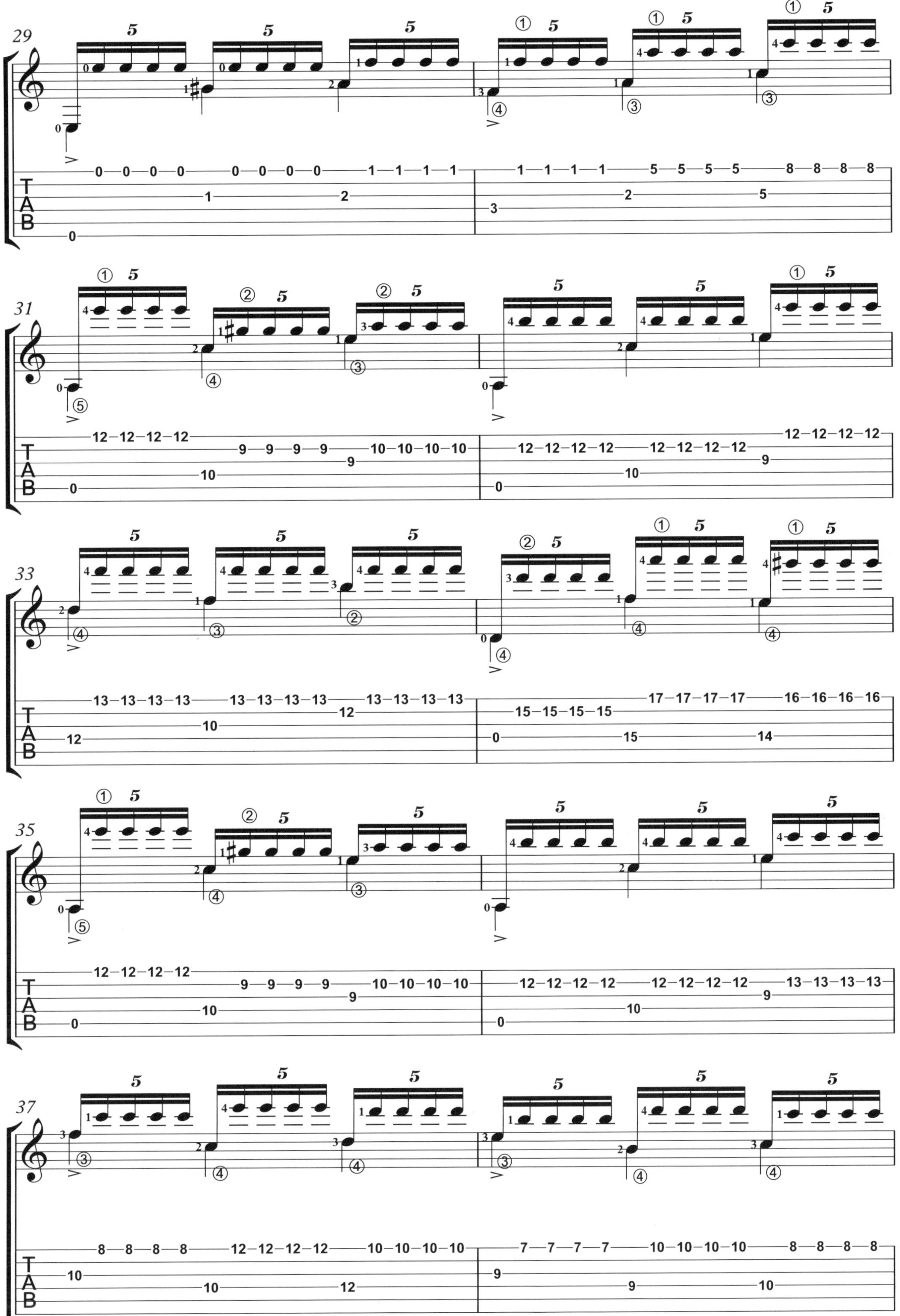

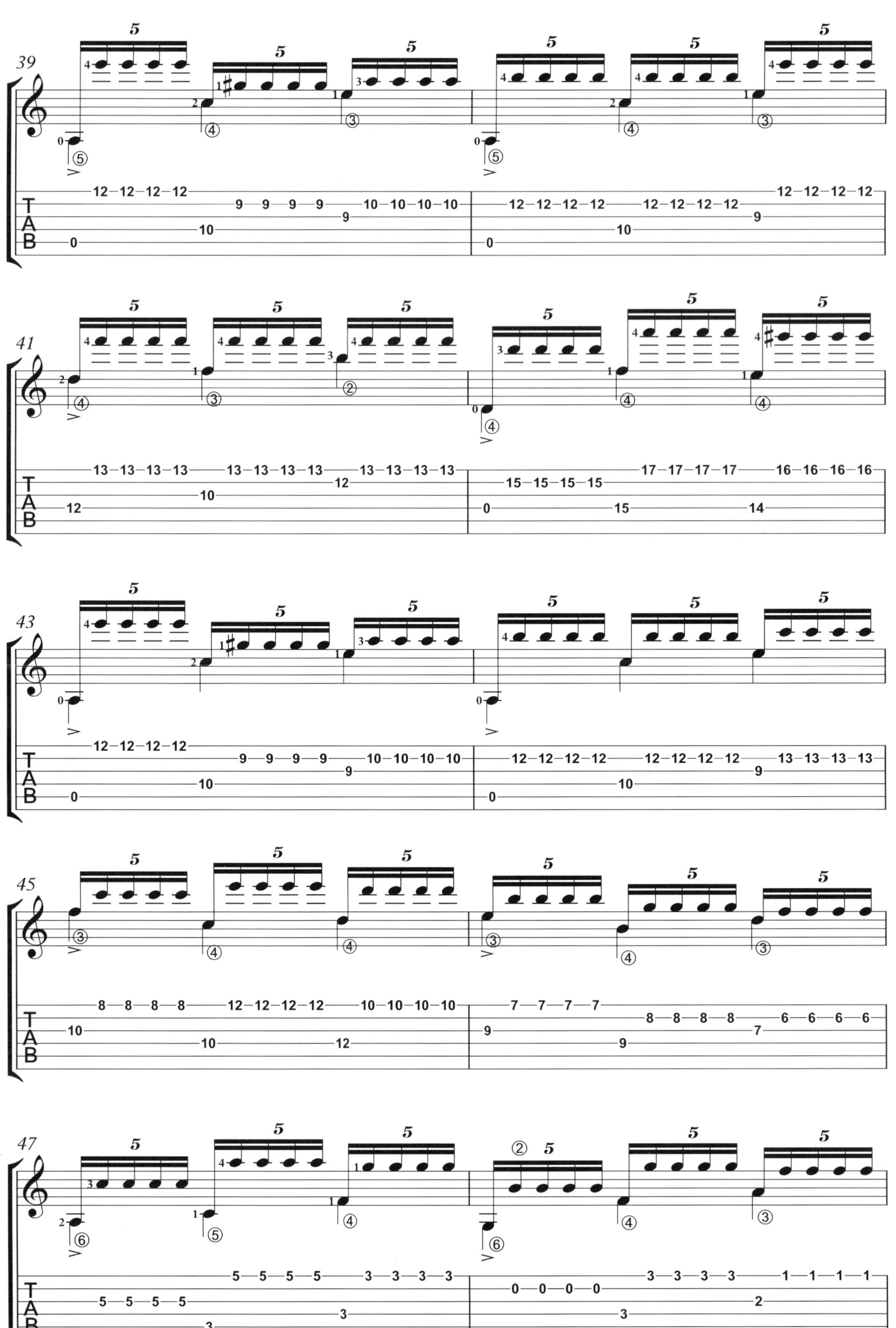
39
41
43
45
47
TAB

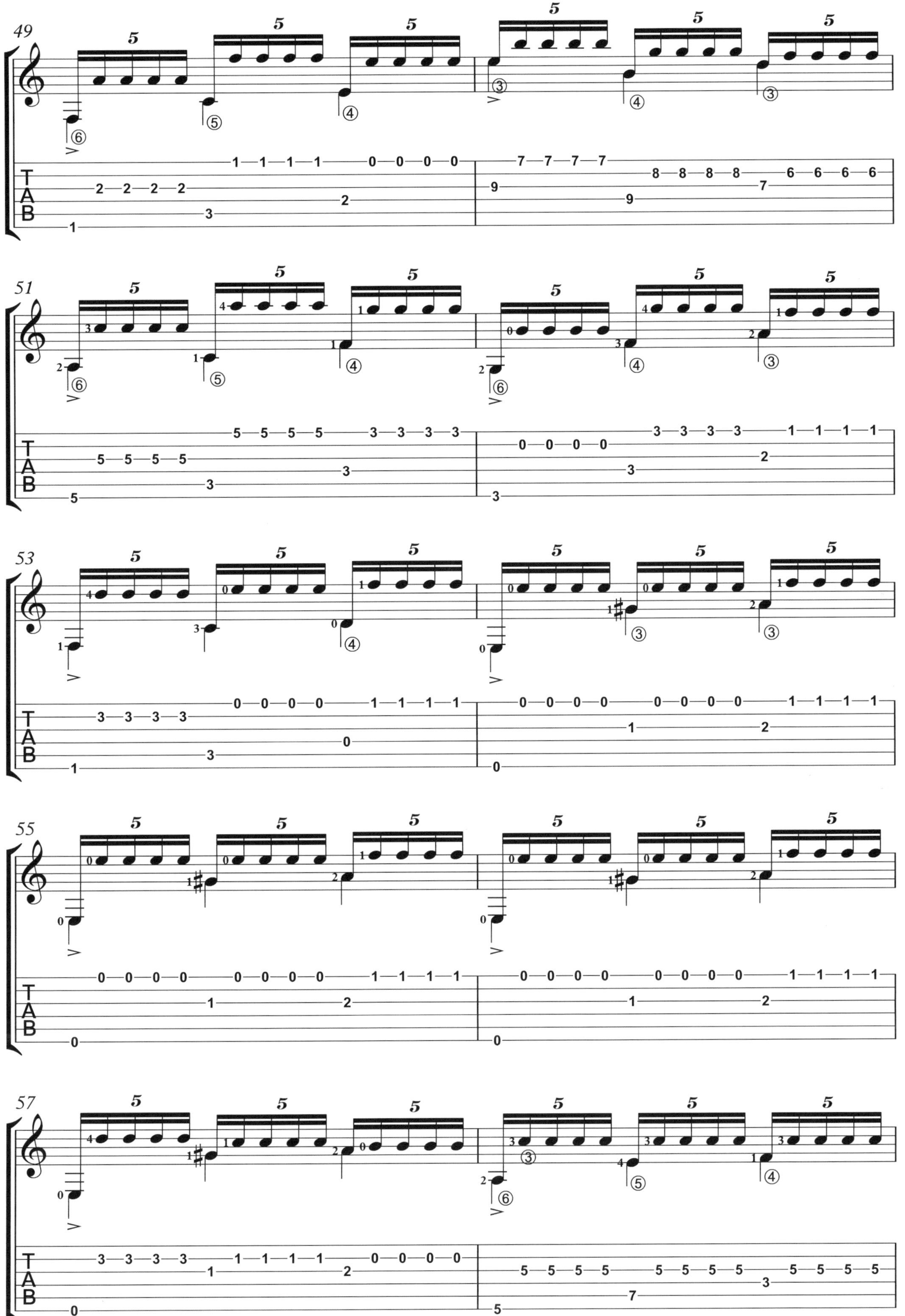

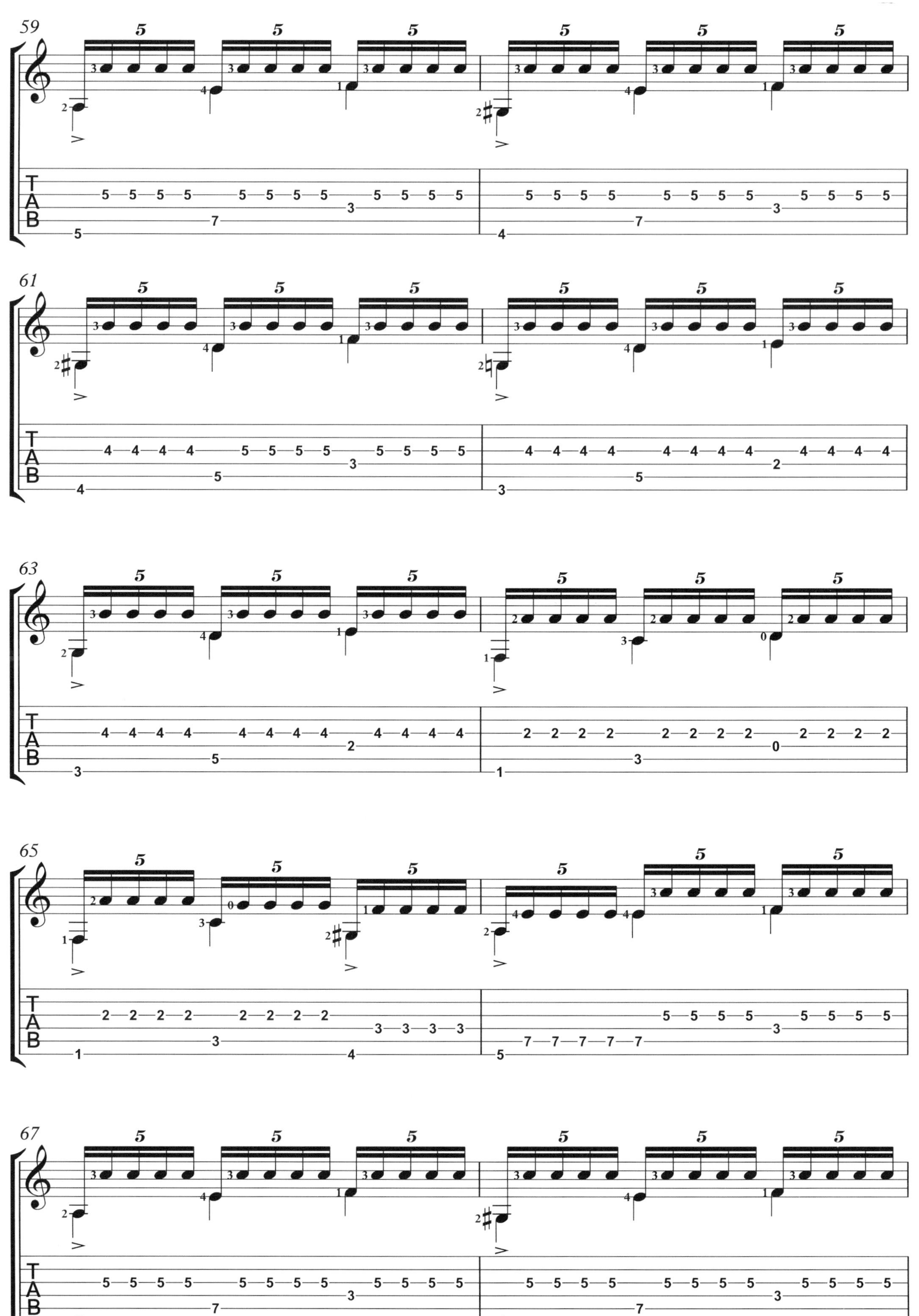

ETUDE XVII

Octave Study

Here is some practice with octaves in E Aeolian.

"Since I retired, I only practice four hours a day."

Julian Bream

Etude XVII

Tempo ♩.=160

Music and transcription by
YAGO SANTOS

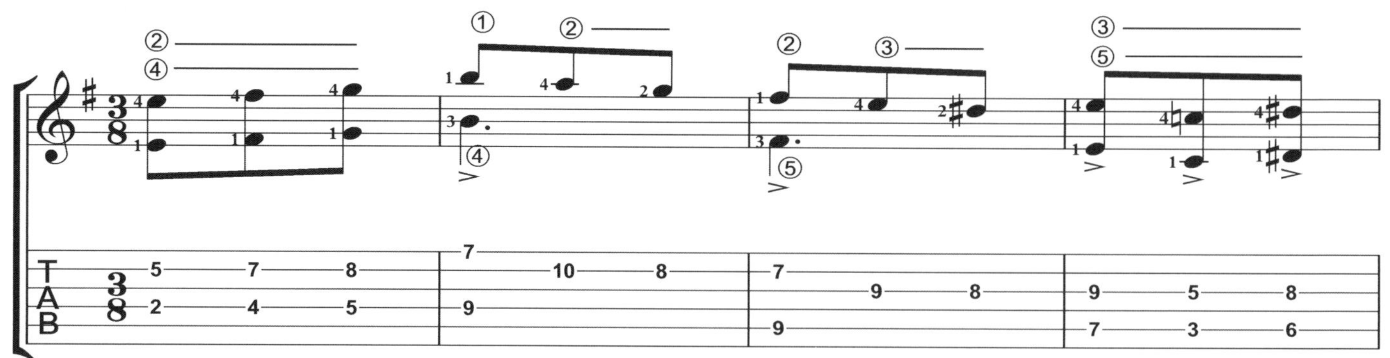

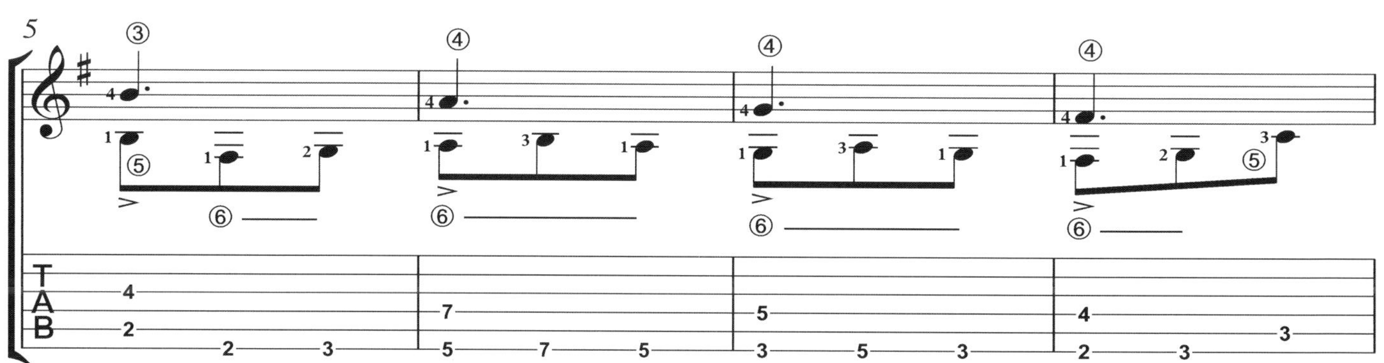

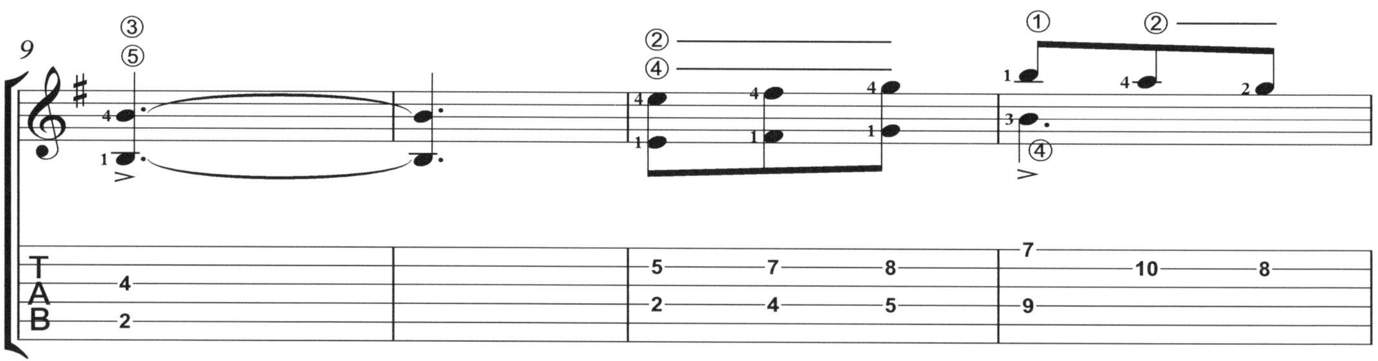

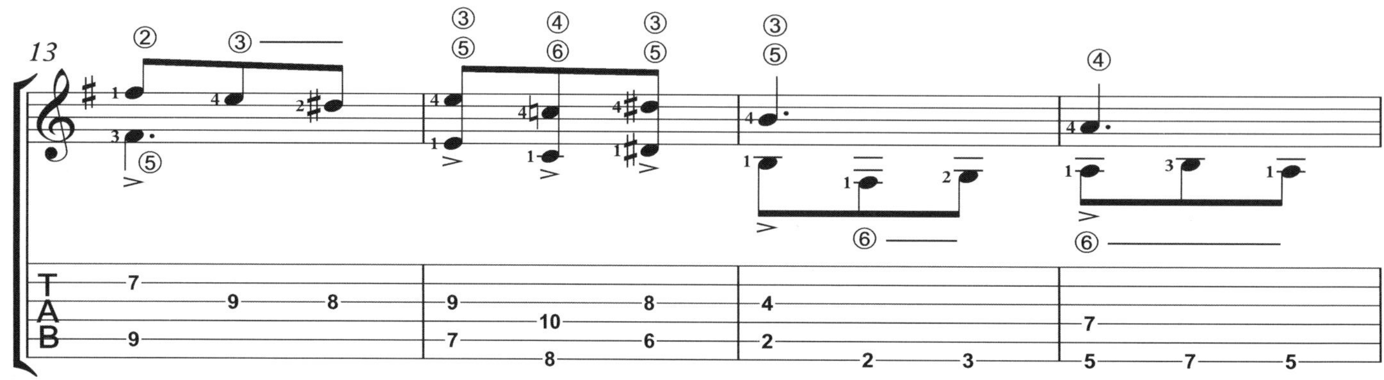

38
42
46
TAB

ETUDE XVIII

Arpeggio Study

This study provides practice with different types of right-hand arpeggio patterns.

"Maybe I don't believe in myself,
but I do believe in what I'm doing."

Jimmy Page

Etude XVIII
Chords

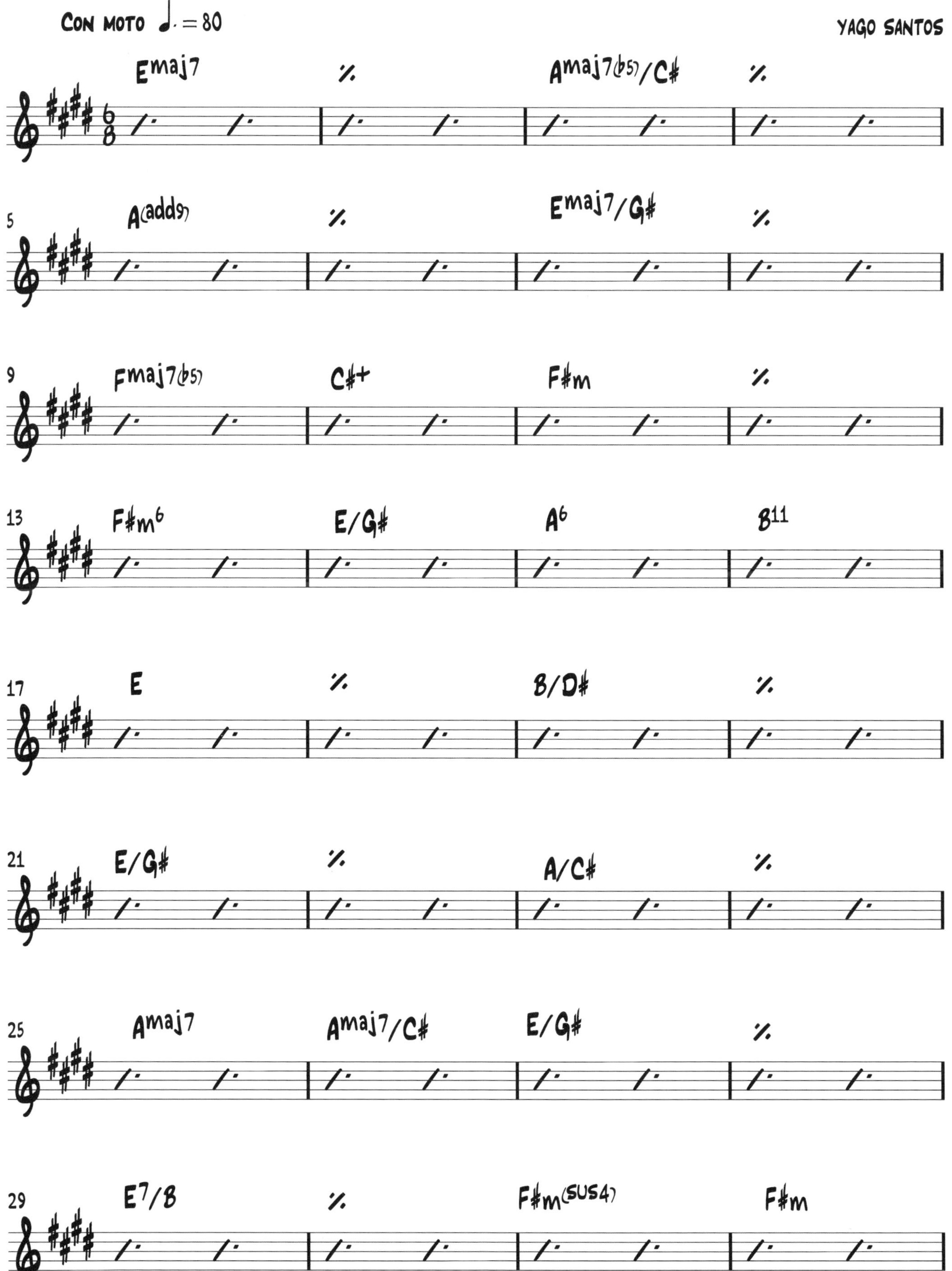

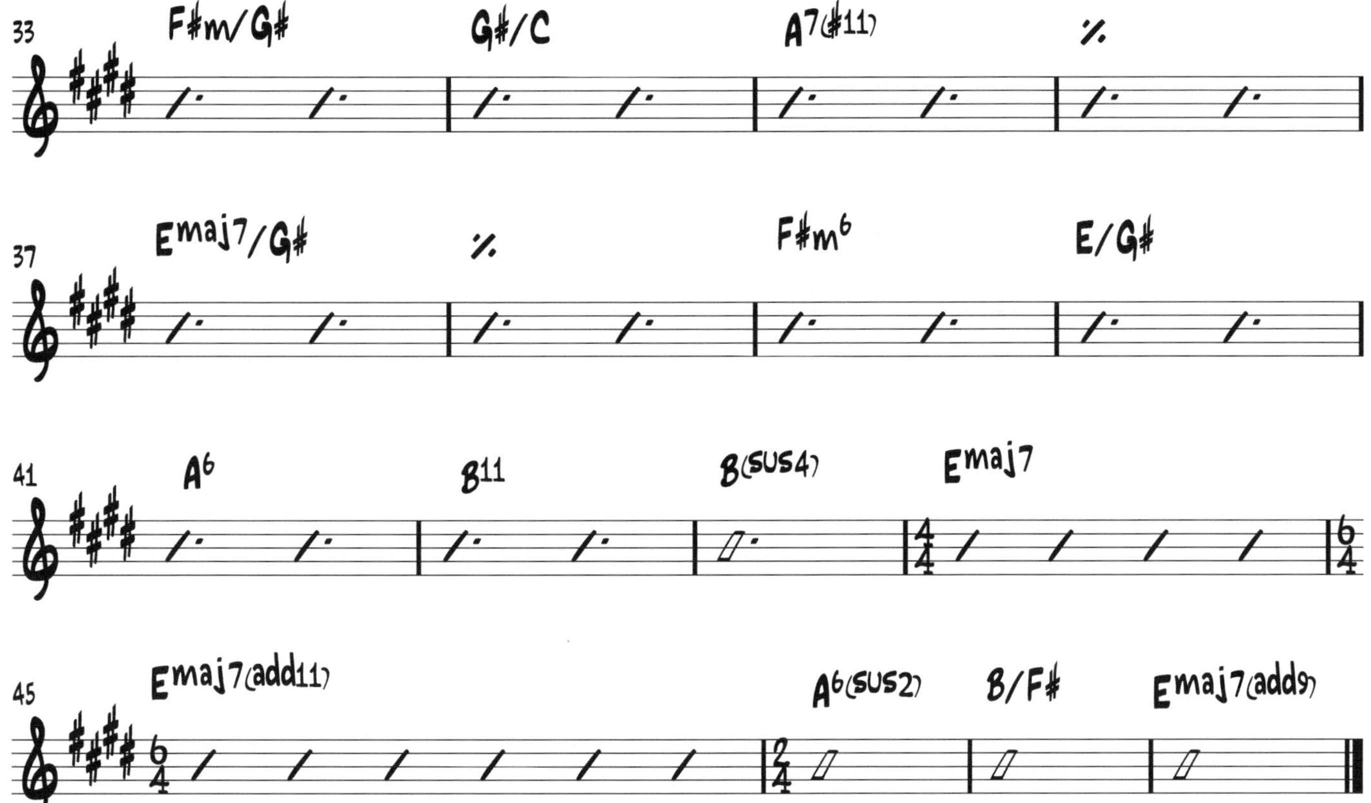
33
F#m/G#
G#/C
A7(#11)
37
Emaj7/G#
F#m6
E/G#
41
A6
B11
B(SUS4)
Emaj7
45
Emaj7(add11)
A6(SUS2)
B/F#
Emaj7(add9)

Etude XVIII

Music and transcription by
YAGO SANTOS

Con moto ♩=80

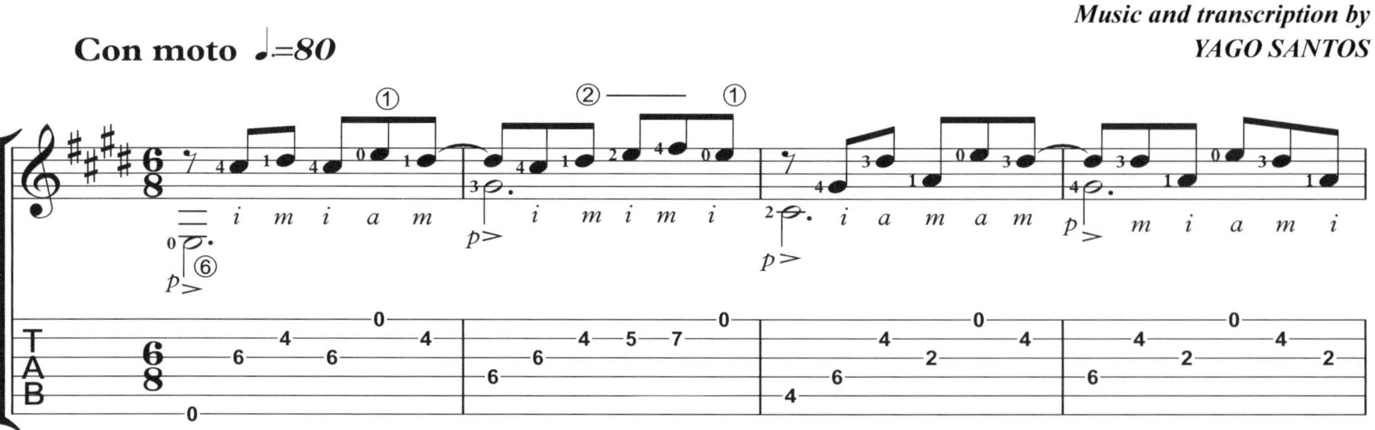

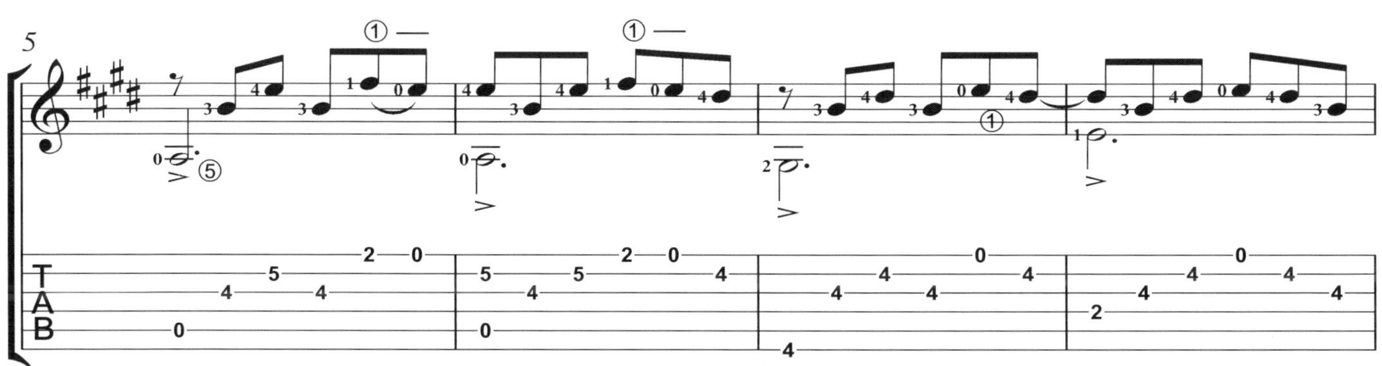

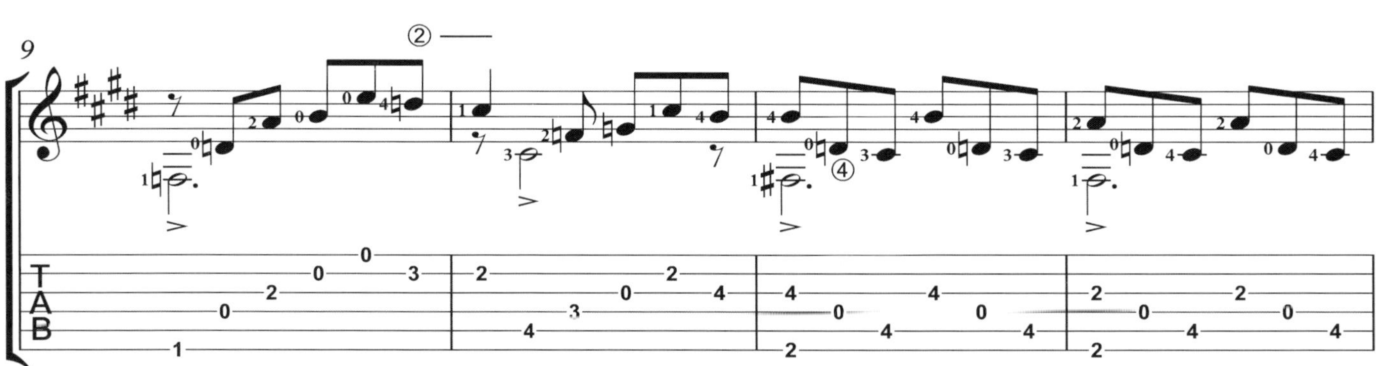

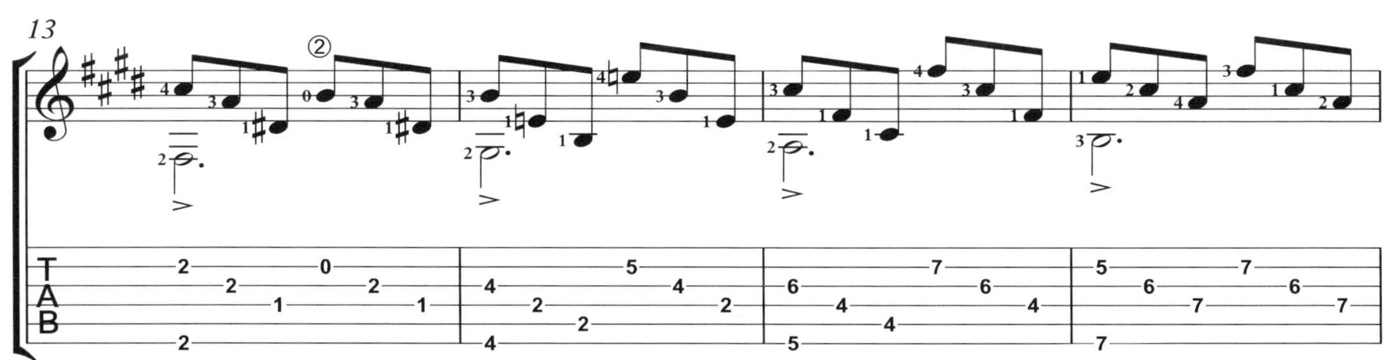

C IX

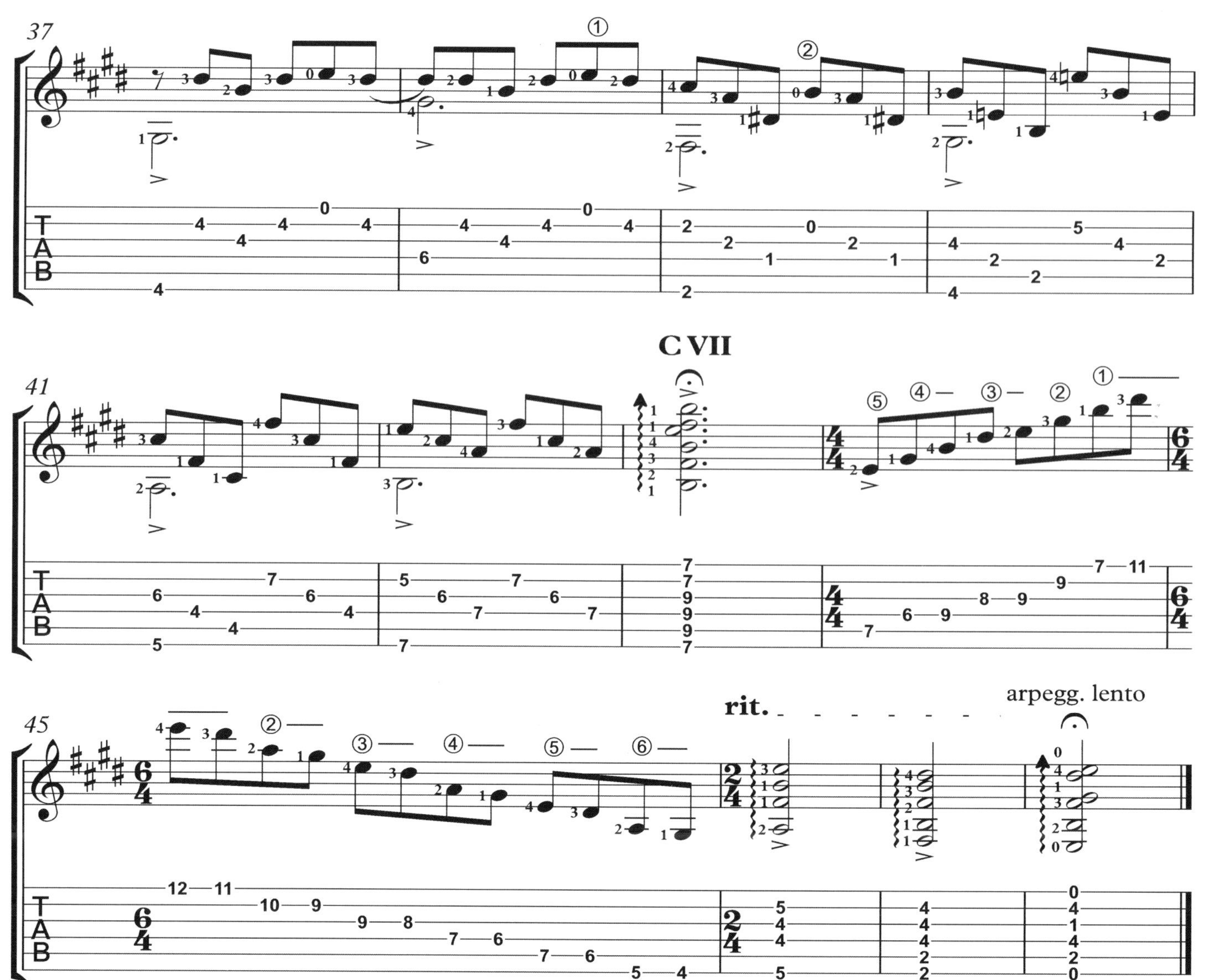
C VII
rit.
arpegg. lento

ETUDE XIX

Horquilla Study

This study requires facility with the *horquilla* technique and the ${}^{a}_{p}$ *i m i p i m i* pattern.

"Looking back, it seems to me that, musically,
I have learned much more from relationships
with people I have met and admired."

John Williams

Etude XIX
Chords

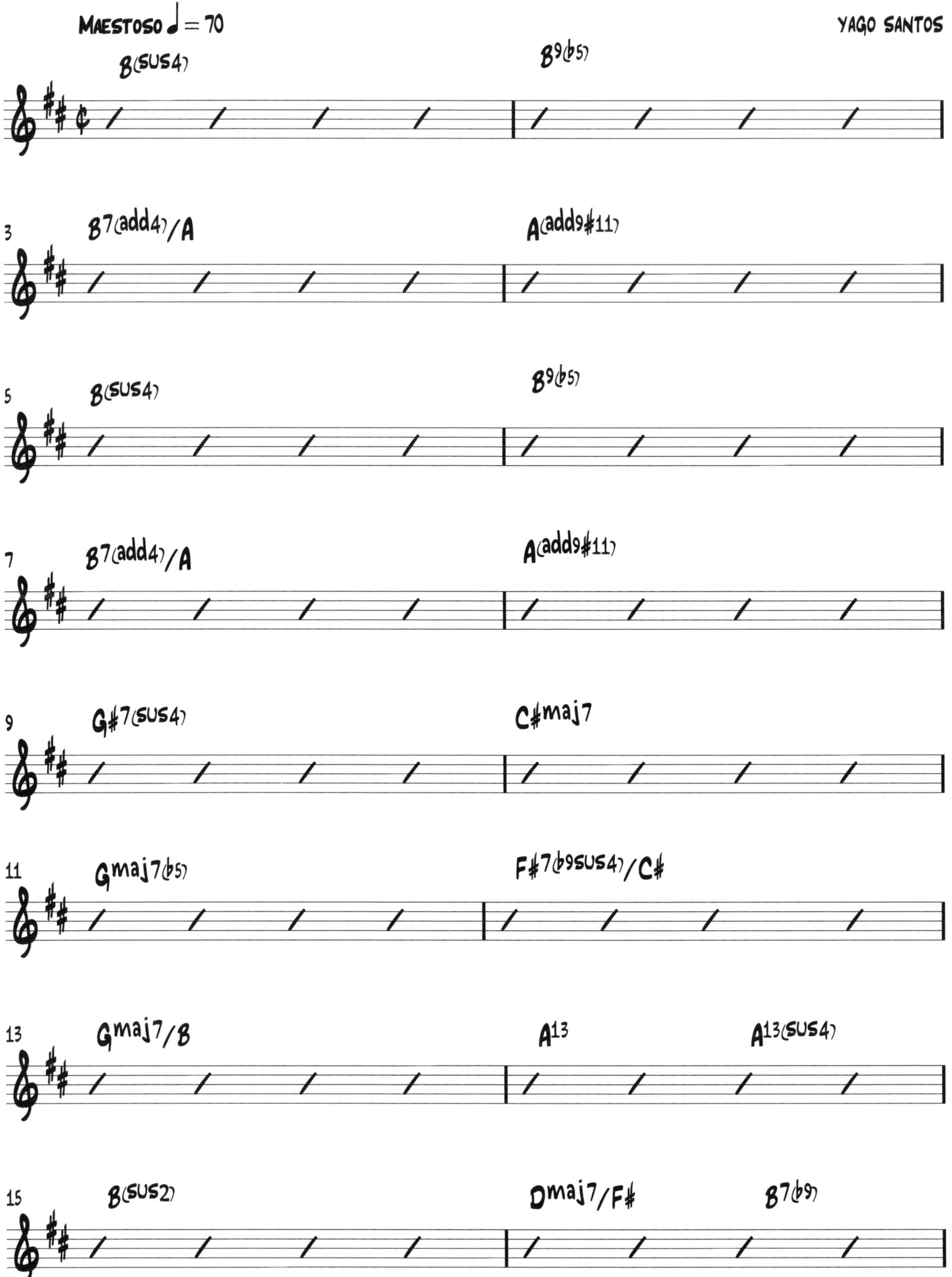

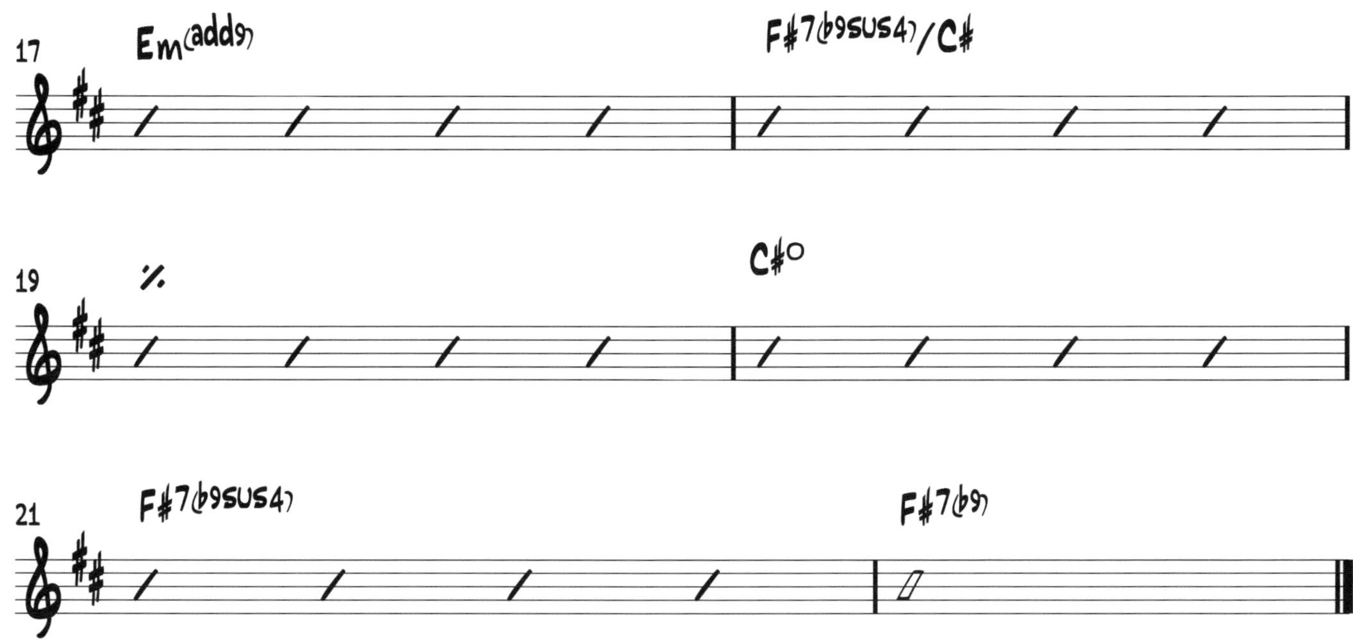
17
Em(add9)
F#7(b9sus4)/C#
19
%
C#o
21
F#7(b9sus4)
F#7(b9)

Etude XIX

Maestoso ♩=70

Music and transcription by
YAGO SANTOS

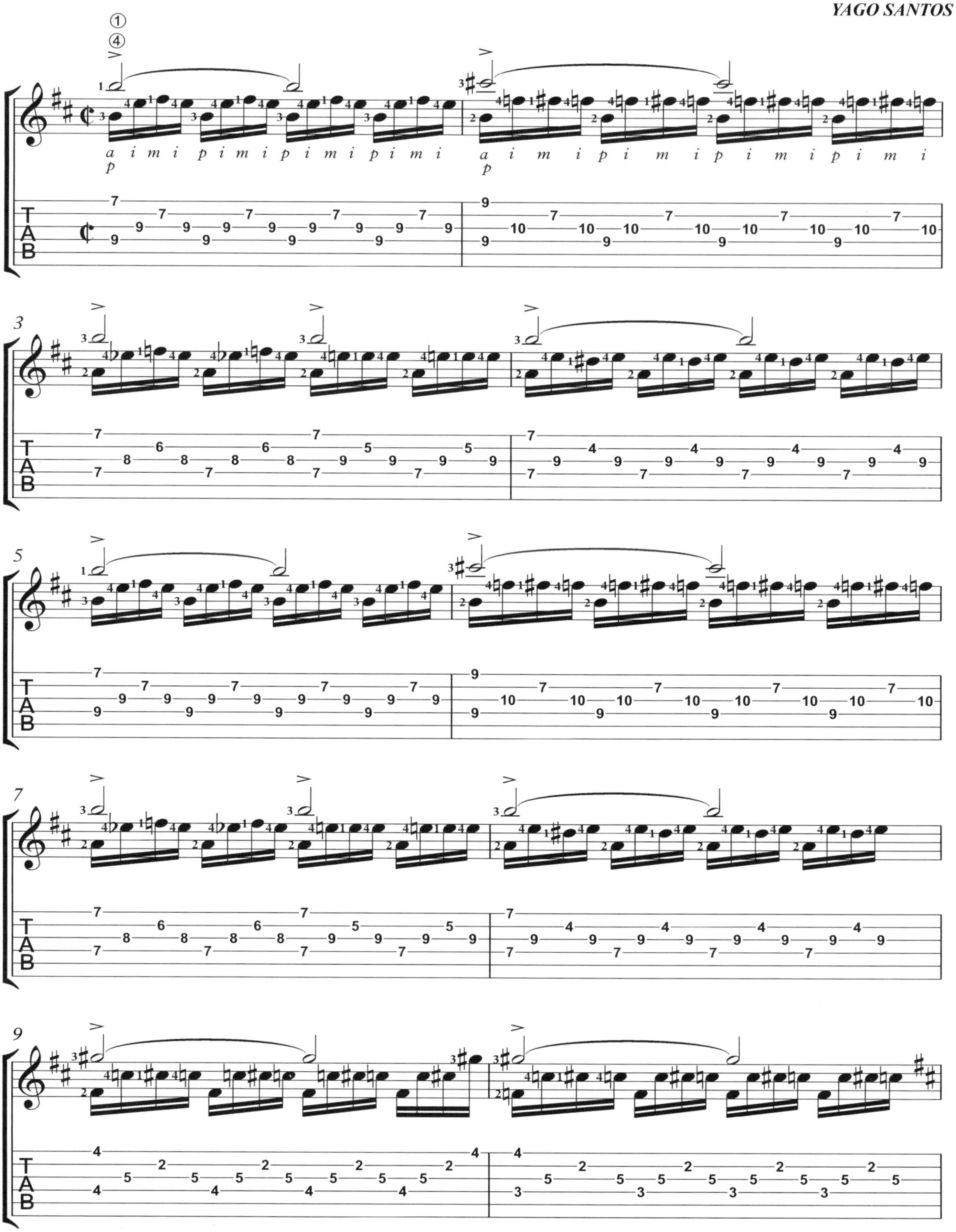

11

13

15

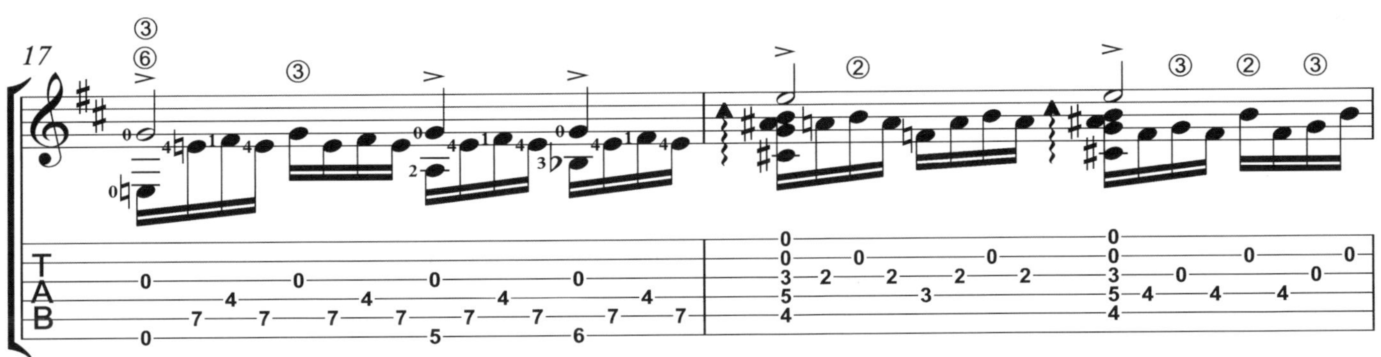

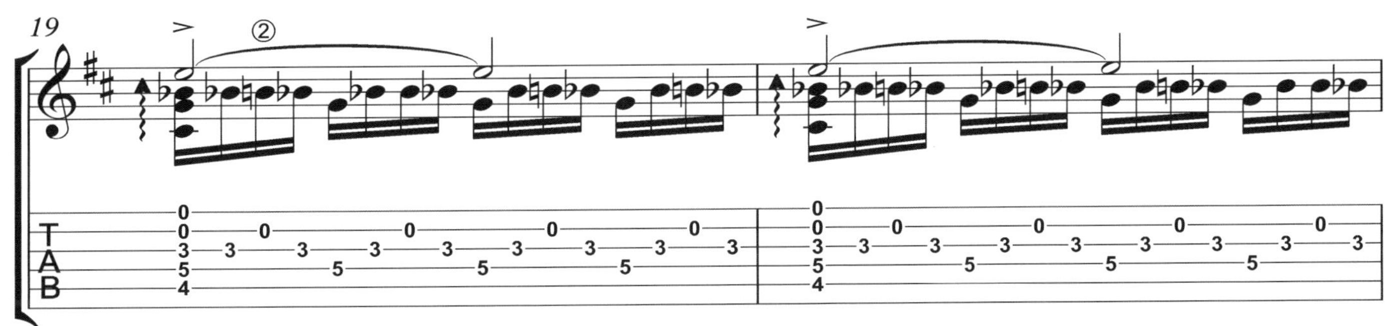

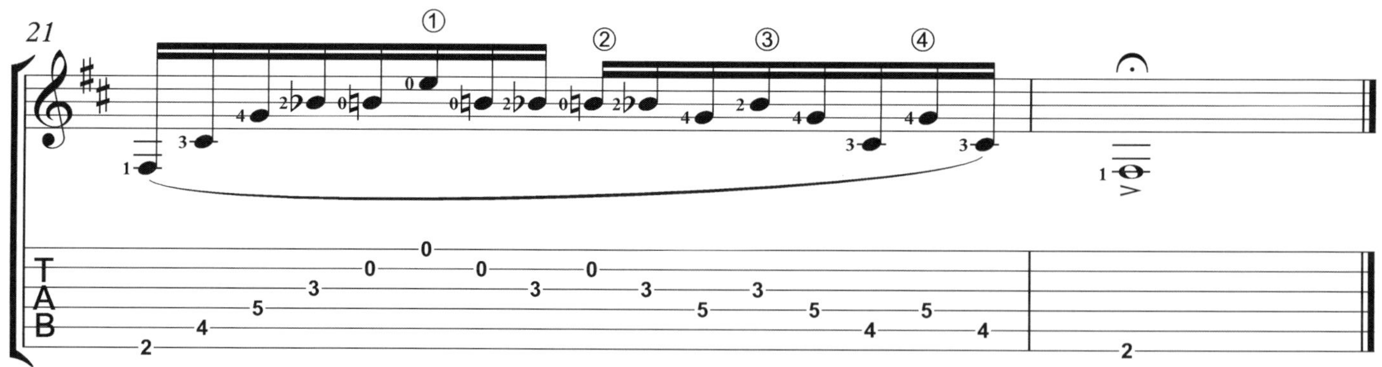

ETUDE XX

Minuet by Rafael Riqueni

This last etude will provide further practice wih picado technique, as well as with ${}^{i}_{p}$ ${}^{m}_{p}$ patterns.

Etude XX
Chords

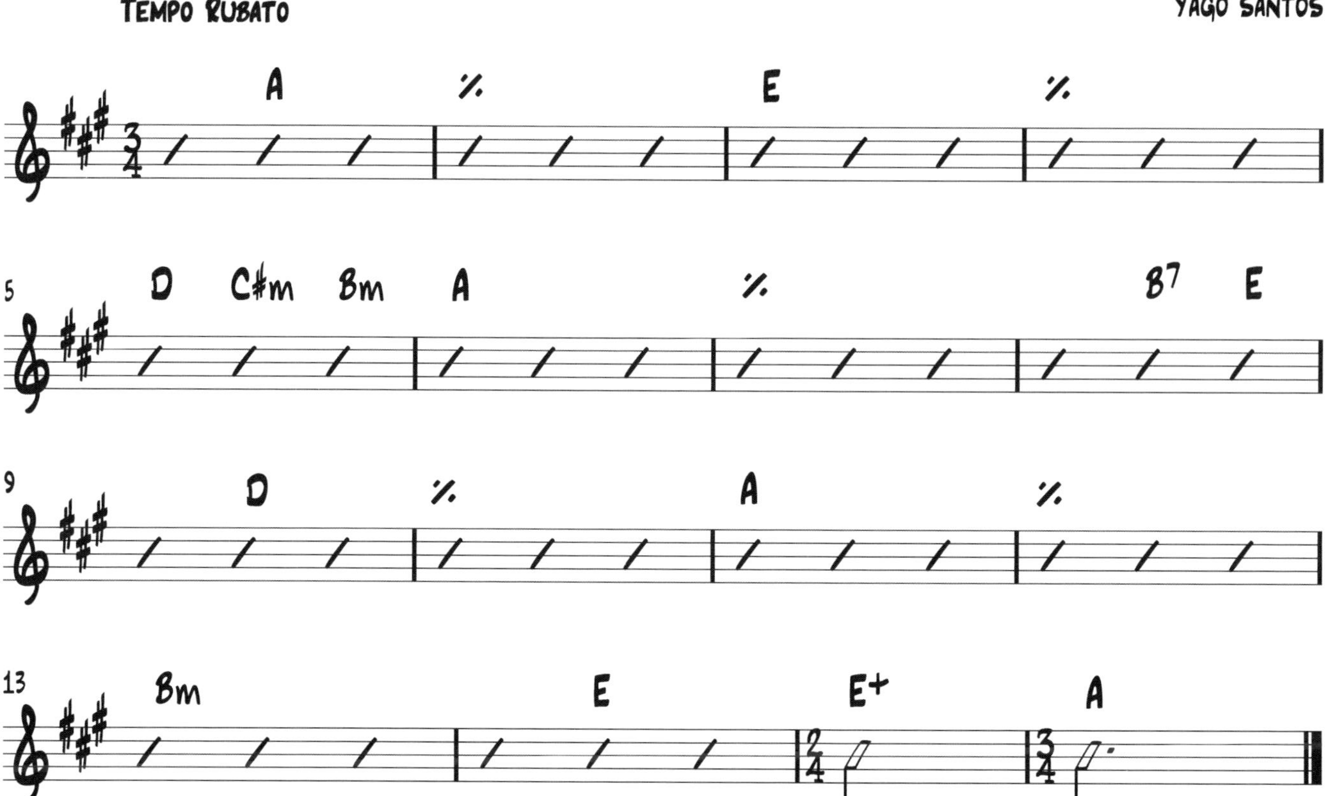

Etude XX

Tempo Rubato

Music by RAFAEL RIQUENI
Transcription by YAGO SANTOS

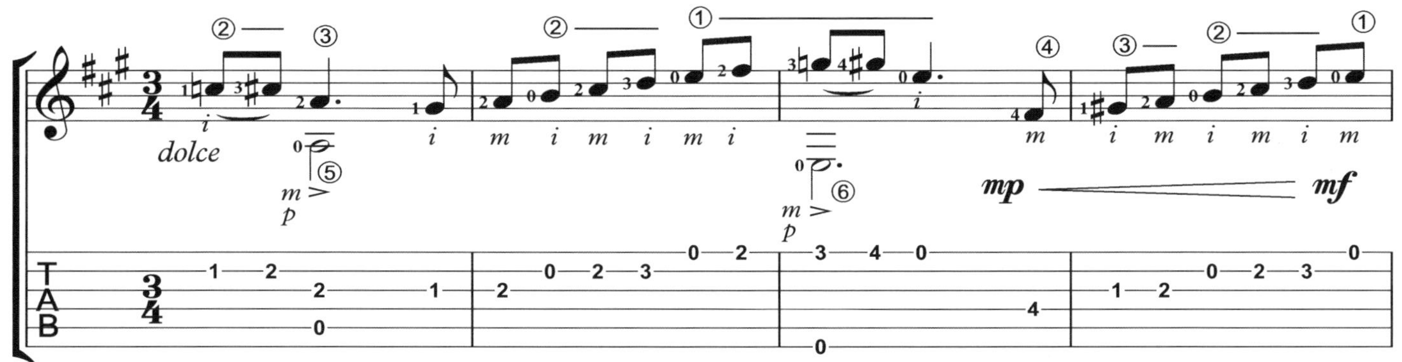

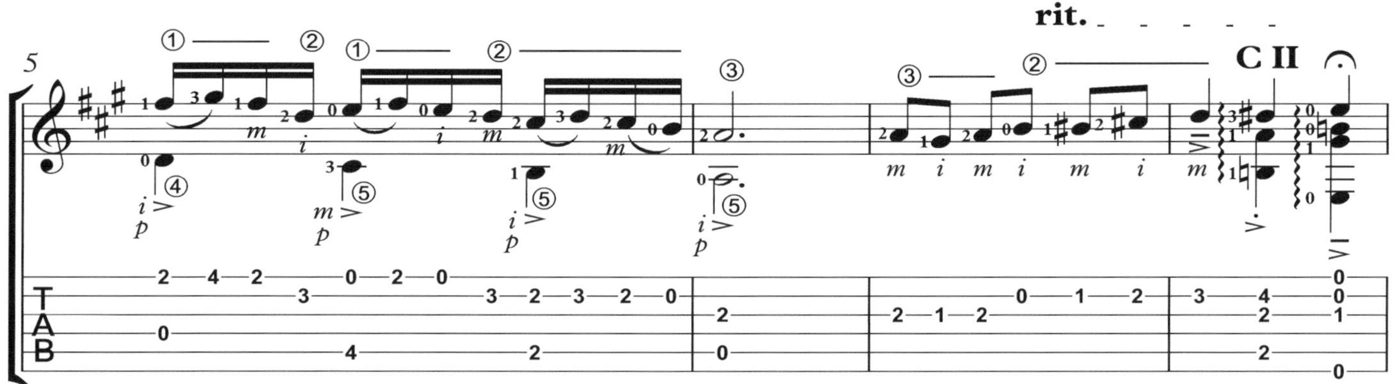

A tempo

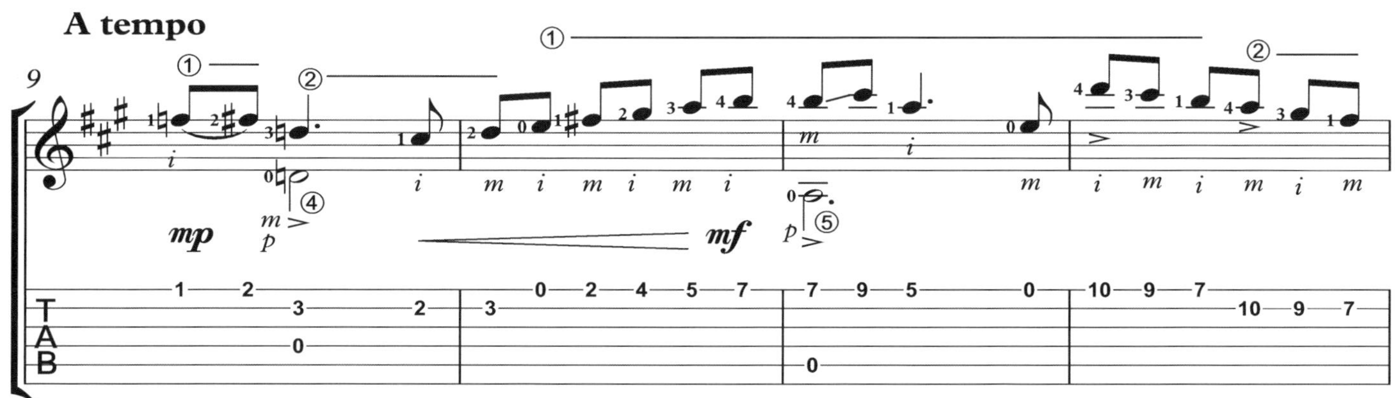

About the Author

Yago Santos
Photo Courtesy of Diego Gallardo López

Born December 28, 1985 and raised in Bilbao (Spain), Yago Santos is a student of the master Rafael Riqueni. He has toured internationally as a soloist and shared stages with flamenco artists such as José Mercé, Manuel Molina, Rafael Riqueni, El Pele, José el de la Tomasa, and Mayte Martín. Yago holds a master's degree from Berklee College of Music, where he received a full scholarship and graduated summa cum laude.

Two months after graduating from Berklee, he won the first International Paco de Lucía Prize at the International Guitar Competition of Seville and collaborated with Hans Zimmer and Lorne Balfe on the EMI nominated series *Genius: Picasso* (*National Geographic*). His first solo album, *Alma de Niño* was released in 2021.

Recommended Listening

Manuel Agujetas, *El Rey del Cante Gitano*, 1997

Remedios Amaya, *Me Voy Contigo*, 1997

Vicente Amigo, *De Mi Corazón al Aire,* 1991

Vicente Amigo, *Vivencias Imaginadas, 1995*

Various artists, *Canta Jerez*, 1967

Various artists, *V.OR.S. Jerez al Cante*, 2012

Various artists, *Antologia del Cante Flamenco,* 1954

Juan Manuel Cañizares, *Noches de Imán y Luna,* 1997

Manolo Caracol, *Lo Mejor de Manolo Caracol, 1979*

Moraíto Chico, *Morao Morao*, 2005

Duquende, *Samaruco*, 2006

Fosforito, *Fosforito en los Cantes del Rincón de Cádiz*, 1979

Manolo Franco, *Aljibe*, 1986

Pepe Habichuela, *A Mandeli,* 1983

Camarón de la Isla, *Potro de Rabia y Miel*, 1991

Carmen Linares, *Antología: La mujer en el cante*, 1996

Dani de Morón, *Cambio de Sentido*, 2012

Josemi Carmona, *Las pequeñas cosas*, 2011

Josemi Carmona y Carles Benavent, *Sumando*, 2006

Recommended Listening

Antonio Mairena, *Grands Cantaores du flamenco*, 2012

Antonio Rey, *A través de tí*, 2007

Pepe Marchena, *Grands Cantaores du flamenco Vol. 10*

Paco de Lucía, *Fuente y Caudal,* 1973

Paco de Lucía, *Siroco,* 1987

Paco de Lucía, *Luzía,* 1998

Juan Peña "El Lebrijano", *Persecución*, 1976

La Macanita, *La Luna de Tomasa*, 2001

Enrique Morente, *Morente sueña la Alhambra*, 2006

Estrella Morente, *Mi cante y un poema,* 2001

Gerardo Núñez, *Andando el Tiempo*, 2004

Enrique de Melchor, *La noche y el día*, 1991

Niño Miguel, *Diferente*, 1976

Victor Monge "Serranito," *Guitarra Flamenca,* 1971

Ramón Montoya, *Grandes Figures du Flamenco Vol. 5,* 1988

Miguel Poveda, *Tierra y Calma*, 2006

Diego del Morao, *Orate*, 2010

El Pele, *Canto*, 2003

Niño Ricardo, *Grandes Figures du Flamenco,* 1991

Recommended Listening

Rafael Riqueni, *Mi Tiempo,* 1990

Juan Carlos Romero, *Romero*, 2004

Juan Carlos Romero, *Agua Encendida,* 2010

Sabicas, *El Rey del Flamenco,* 1965

Manolo Sanlúcar, *Tauromagia,* 1988

Tomatito, *Guitarra Gitana*, 1996

El Viejín, *Algo que Decir*, 1999

La Niña de los Peines, *Arte Flamenco Vol. 7 (1890-1969)*

Diego el Cigala, *Corren tiempos de alegría*, 2001

Mayte Martín, *Querencia*, 2000

Manolo Caracol, *Fandangos Caracoleros*, 1958

Niño Josele, *Niño Josele*, 2002

Rafael Riqueni, *Alcázar de Cristal*, 1996

Manuel Torre, *Grabaciones históricas, 1909-1931*

Juan Habichuela, *De la Zambra al Duende*, 2008

Glossary of Terms

A

abanico - literally "fan." Refers to a subcategory of rasgueo, using either *p, e, i* and *p, m*. Alternative methods include *p, ma* or *p, a, i*.
abandolao - a flamenco style that originated in Málaga
abeto - fir tree
acento - accent
a compás - in rhythm
acompañamiento - comping
acorde - chord
aficionado - someone that is interested in flamenco music.
afinador - tuner. From spanish afinar, "to tune."
aflamencado - "flamenco-ized"
al aire - open (string)
anular - ring finger (notated as "*a*")
a palo seco - group of *palos* performed by a cantaor without guitar accompaniment.
apoyando - from Spanish "apoyar" meaning "support." Strings are struck towards the soundboard in such way that the striking finger is caught and supported by the next string.
aros - sides of the guitar
arpeggio - plucking individual notes of a chord, e.g., *p, i, m, a, m, i*
arrastre - glissé or slide
arreglo - arrangement

B

bailaor - male flamenco dancer
bailaora - female flamenco dancer
baile - flamenco dance
bajañí - flamenco term for "guitar"
bajo - bass
bambera - a flamenco style derived from Andalusian folklore.
bemol - flat
blanca - literally "white," a flamenco guitar made of cypress.
boca - sound hole of the guitar
bordones - three lowest strings of the guitar (4, 5, 6)

C

cabeza - "head" of the flamenco guitar
cadencia - cadence
café cantante - literally "singing café". A bar or club where flamenco musicians sang at the beginning of the second half of the XIX century.
caja - sound box of the guitar
cajón - percussion instrument, originally from Perú, basically a hollow wooden box with a sound hole and snares. Introduced to flamenco music by Paco de Lucía during one of his tours of that country.
cantar - to sing
cantaor - male flamenco singer
cantaora - female flamenco singer
cante - flamenco singing

cante gitano - gypsy style of flamenco singing
cante jondo - pure flamenco singing, a.k.a. – "deep song"
cantiñas - flamenco style typical of Cádiz
cedro - cedar
cejilla - barré, the stopping of all or several strings at the same fret by the index finger of the fretting hand/capo.
chasqueo - buzzing
cierre - last or "closing" measure of a *remate*
clavijero - tuning peg
coletilla - tag, short refrain at the end of a flamenco stanza
compás - beat, rhythm, measure; a flamenco guitarist must have a sense of compás.
copla - literally "couplet." A type of stanza or estrofa used in flamenco literature. Each copla is usually three or four verses (tercios) long, with octosyllabic lines.
couplé - couple, a type of buleria style
cromática - chromatic
cuadro - literally "painting." Flamenco musicians use this word to refer to a group of flamenco performers, including the dancer, singer and guitar player.
cuerda - string

D

decir - to say or to sing
derecha - right hand (i.e., strumming hand)
desplante - gypsy pose; a sudden, showy movement which may appear out of musical context.
detalle - literally "detail," much shorter than a falseta, generally one or a half measure long.
diapasón - fingerboard of the guitar
digitación - fingering
duende - spirited yet gracious quality of a very good flamenco performance.

E

ébano - ebony
ejercicio - exercise
escala - scale
escuela - school
escobilla - literally "broom." Concrete inner-structure of passages in certain palos/bailes, such as soleá or alegrías.
estrofa - stanza, a section of a lyric

F

falseta - a prepared or improvised guitar-focused variation.
fandango - a type of flamenco style
fiesta - party
fondo - back of the guitar

G

grave - bass tone
golpe - literally, a "hit" or tap on the sound box.
golpeador - tap guard
guajira - a type of flamenco style from South America
guitarrero - guitar builder

H

hacia abajo - downward
hacia arriba - upward
horquilla - a right-hand arpeggio technique in which we use the fingerings *p/i/m/i* or *p/m/a/m*.
hueso - saddle of the guitar

I

índice - index finger (notated as "*i*")
izquierda - left hand (i.e., fretboard hand)

J

jaleo - shouts of encouragement to cheer the performers in a flamenco show ("olé" or "vamos allá" are the most frequent jaleos).
Jondo - literally "Deep". Refers to pure flamenco
juerga - Flamenco party

L

letras - lyrics/words
llamada - literally, "call." Specific set of footwork that lets the dancer communicate with the singer and the guitar player that a change or an ending is coming.
ligado - slur
lutier - Also "guitarrero". Guitar builder

M

mano - hand
mástil - fretboard
mayor - major (key)
media cejilla - semi-barré
medio - middle finger (notated as "*m*")
menor - minor (key)
meñique - little finger (notated as "*e*")

N

negra - literally, "black." Flamenco guitar made of dark rosewood as opposed to a *rubia* (blonde) made of light-colored cypress.
nudillos - knuckles

P

palmas - rhythmic hand claps that accompany a flamenco performance.
palo - flamenco song/form (e.g., solea, tangos, bulerias, alegrias, etc.)
pellizco - literally, "nip, pinch." An artist's or performance's distinctive sense of infectious rhythm.
picado - playing single note melodies using i, m or m, i. Alternative methods include *i, a* and *m, a*.
pie - foot
por arriba - E Phrygian tonality
por medio - A Phrygian tonality

posición - the position or setting of the fingers of the fretting hand for playing of a chord, arpegio, or passage.
posturas - flamenco guitarist term for "chords"
primas - the first three strings of the guitar
puente - bridge of the flamenco guitar
pulgar - thumb (notated as "*p*")
pulgar/índice - thumb/index
pulsación - the action or "feel" of the guitar strings; in flamenco music, this term also refers to the rhythmic feel and sound of a guitar player.

R

rajeo - (also rasgueo or rasgueado) the strumming of chords peculiar to the flamenco guitar in ascending or descending order of notes.
remate - the last couple of measures of a falseta or of a particular baile or cante.
resonancia - resonance
rumba - a type of flamenco style typical in Cataluña.

S

soniquete - literally "droning." Flamenco rhythm mastery.
sorda - deaf
sostenido - sharp

T

tablao - bar or club with a stage for flamenco shows
tango - a type of flamenco style
tanguillo - a type of flamenco style originating in Cádiz
tapa armónica - top of the flamenco guitar, soundboard
taranta - a type of flamenco style coming from Almería
templar - to tune
tercio - literally "thirds." Each single verse or musical phrase of a flamenco song.
tiempos - beats
tirando - free or unsupported plucking strokes
tocaor - flamenco guitarist
tocar - to play
tono - "pitch" or "key"
toque - the art of flamenco guitar playing
trastes - frets of the guitar
trémolo - strumming hand technique that consists of playing one bass note and three or four upper notes with the following fingering: pami or *p*, *i*, *a*, *m*, *i*.

U

uñas - fingernails

Z

zambra - a type of flamenco guitar style and dance
zapateado - footwork/dance

Other Mel Bay Spanish Guitar Books and Books by Yago Santos

16 Modern Studies for Flamenco Guitar (Santos)
Music of Debussy for Solo Guitar (Santos)
Andalucian Suite No. 1 (J. Martin)
Classical and Flamenco Guitar Solos and Etudes (Elysa Hochman/Jason Hochman)
Easy Flamenco Solos (Agen)
Easy to Play Flamenco and Classical Guitar Solos (Hochman)
Flamenco Guitar Solos Vol. 1 (Marraccini)
Flamenco Guitar Solos Vol. 2 (Marraccini)
Flamenco Music for Acoustic Guitar (Agen)
Guitarra Solista (Juan Martin)
Juan Serrano: Flamenco Concert Selections
Juan Serrano: Flamenco Guitar Solos
Juan Serrano: King of the Flamenco Guitar
Sabicas (de la Mata)
12 Spanish Dances by Granados (Griggs)
Classical and Flamenco Guitar Solos and Etudes (E. Hochman/J. Hochman)
Carmen Suite (Ausqui)
Easy to Play Flamenco and Classical Guitar Solos (Hochman)
España: Opus 165 by Albeniz (Griggs)
Granados: Romantic and Poetic Scenes (Griggs)
Isaac Albeniz: 26 Pieces Arranged for Guitar (S. Yates)
Definitive de Falla (Ausqui)
Ernesto Cordero: Two Popular Andalusian Themes
Guitarra Solista (Juan Martin)
Romance Variations (Stover)
Selected Works of Enrique Granados for Solo Guitar (Barreiro)
Spanish Composers for Classical Guitar (Afshar)
Spanish Dance No. 5: Andaluza by Enrique Granados arr. by Pepe Romero
Treasures of the Spanish Guitar (DeChiaro)
Valses Poeticos by Enrique Granados (Afshar)
Essential Flamenco Guitar Vol. 1 (J. Martin/Campbell)
Essential Flamenco Guitar Vol. 2. (J. Martin/Campbell)
Flamenco Classical Guitar Tradition (J. Serrano/Whitehead)
Juan Serrano: Flamenco Guitar/Basic Techniques
Play Solo Flamenco Guitar with Juan Martin Vol. 1
Play Solo Flamenco Guitar with Juan Martin Vol. 2
The Keys to Flamenco Guitar Vol. 1 (Koster)

WWW.MELBAY.COM